D0252472

PATTERNS
OF
PROTESTANT
CHURCH MUSIC

PATTERNS
OF
PROTESTANT
CHURCH MUSIC

BY

ROBERT M. STEVENSON

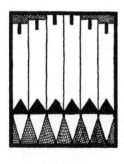

DUKE UNIVERSITY
PRESS   1953

LIBRARY
MAR 5 1968
UNIVERSITY OF THE PACIFIC

179729

COPYRIGHT, 1953, BY THE DUKE UNIVERSITY PRESS
ENGLAND: CAMBRIDGE UNIVERSITY PRESS, LONDON, N.W. I
Library of Congress Catalog Card Number 53-8271

THIRD PRINTING, 1965

*Printed in the United States of America By the Seeman
Printery, Inc., Durham, N. C.*

PREFACE

THIS BOOK HAS BEEN WRITTEN IN order to trace the differing musical traditions that have grown up in the various denominations. It has been written for church musicians, many of whom serve in denominations with whose musical traditions they have not familiarized themselves. It has been written also for pastors and other religious leaders charged with promoting denominational interests.

Each of the major denominations has its own appropriate musical traditions, to forsake which impoverishes rather than enriches it. The author wishes from the outset to be understood as favoring the preservation of all those cultural elements in each denominational tradition which are peculiarly its own. This book has not been written with the purpose of magnifying one musical tradition over another, but rather with the purpose of summoning musicians to their duty of respecting and cherishing the traditions in whatever denomination they serve.

If it should seem that considerable space has been devoted to hymns and to the textual problems that have confronted such hymnists as Watts and the Wesleys, the author would remind the church musician that "in the beginning was the word" as far as hymns are concerned. Certainly hymns because of their first place in any order of Protestant worship deserve extensive treatment in any history of Protestant music.

For assistance during the writing of this book the author wishes to thank Dr. and Mrs. John Finley

Williamson, eminent founders of the Westminster Choir College; Chaplain (Colonel) Arthur Carl Piepkorn, formerly Commandant of the United States Army Chaplain School; and Drs. Charles R. Erdman, Norman Vincent Hope, and Lefferts Loetscher, professors at the Princeton Theological Seminary. Thanks are also due the Editors of the *Anglican Theological Review*, the *Crozer Quarterly*, the *Harvard Theological Review*, the *Journal of Religion* (University of Chicago), the *Lutheran Quarterly*, *Religion in Life*, and the *Review of Religion* (Columbia University), for permission to reprint material in their copyright ownership.

R. S.

CONTENTS

PREFACE   v

I. LUTHER'S MUSICAL ACHIEVEMENT   3

II. REFORMED CHURCH MUSIC:
The Basic Implications of Calvin's
Philosophy of Church Music   13

III. JOHN MERBECKE AND THE FIRST
ENGLISH PRAYER BOOK   24

IV. BACH'S RELIGIOUS ENVIRONMENT:
The Wellsprings of Religious Emotion That
Nourished His Creative Life   41

V. J. S. BACH'S "APPEALS TO CAESAR"   56

VI. BACH'S QUARREL WITH THE REC-
TOR OF ST. THOMAS SCHOOL   67

VII. HANDELIAN ORATORIO   78

VIII. DR. WATTS'S "FLIGHTS OF FANCY"   93

IX. JOHN WESLEY'S FIRST HYMNBOOK   112

X. THE MUSICAL WESLEYS:
The Flowering of Musical Genius in the
Wesley Family of the Second and Third
Generations   131

XI. JOHN MASON NEALE AND TRAC-
    TARIAN HYMNODY   139

XII. IRA D. SANKEY AND THE GROWTH
     OF "GOSPEL HYMNODY"   151

    APPENDICES   163

        I. Twentieth-Century Papal Pronouncements
           on Music: The Impact of Papal Teaching
           in the United States   165

       II. The Jewish *Union Hymnal*   177

    BIBLIOGRAPHY   187

    INDEX   197

PATTERNS
OF
PROTESTANT
CHURCH MUSIC

I. LUTHER'S MUSICAL ACHIEVEMENT

LUTHER PROCLAIMED AS DID NO OTHER religious leader of his century the value of music in church life. Music in his scale of values ranked second only to theology itself. Something of a performer and a composer himself, he strove tirelessly for superior quality in evangelical music.

During his later career he became ever more bitter in attacking Roman usages which seemed to him impurities; but however vehement he became in denouncing them, he never for a moment classified the music of the Roman church in the list of offending practices. Other reformers violently protested against the patterns of musical life which were current in the sixteenth-century Catholic church and occasionally (as with Zwingli) sought to banish all concerted music from the reformed church because of its corrupt Roman associations.

At Zürich under Zwingli's influence the magistrates in 1524 decreed that there should be "no more playing of organs in the city and in the churches,"[1] and therefore soon afterwards the organ of the Great Minster was broken to pieces. In 1525 all choral singing was discontinued at Zürich in order to allow more time for "prophesyings."[2] In greater or lesser degree than

[1] B. J. Kidd (ed.), *Documents Illustrative of the Continental Reformation* (Oxford, 1911), p. 443.
[2] *Ibid.*, pp. 448-449.

Zwingli, other leaders such as Carlstadt, Farel, Bucer, and Bullinger, not to mention Calvin (whose philosophy of church music we shall later treat separately), opposed organ playing and polyphonic singing in church.

Luther, on the other hand, since he consistently championed not only congregational singing but also the kind of elaborate polyphonic music that only trained choirs can perform, ran counter to the prevailing tendency among reformers. Because he so strenuously exerted himself in behalf of music, his philosophy of church music seems today considerably more attractive to most musicians than does that of any other sixteenth-century Protestant leader.

The specific reasons that make Luther's principles of church music seem attractive today may be listed, and then documented and examined: (1) he showed admirable discrimination in his own evaluation of contemporary composers and thus set a standard of correct musical judgment; (2) he defined music as an art which to be appreciated properly must be studied rather than merely listened to; (3) he made music study a mandatory part of the curriculum in all schools organized under his auspices; (4) he required the ministers who followed his lead to study singing and made an understanding of music a prerequisite to ordination; (5) he overrode the scruples of those who, following St. Augustine's example, feared elaborate church music on moral grounds; (6) he spoke often and ardently in behalf of excellence in church music; (7) while exalting the role of the congregation he never minimized

the role of the organist or of the choir in church music;
(8) he upheld the right of musicians to an adequate and
assured income from church sources.

Documentation for these aspects of his philosophy
is easy to assemble, not only because he wrote so specifically in praise of music, but also because the very obviousness of his interest in church music has attracted
the attention of all Luther scholars. In 1946, for
example, on the four hundredth anniversary of his
death, an important article appeared in which more
than twenty extensive quotations from Luther on the
subject of music were gathered.[3] And two years later
a book appeared, entitled *Luther and Music*.[4]

Because Luther's knowledge of the craft and technique of music composition exceeded that of a mere
dilettante, he was able to make his own musical judgments with remarkable prescience. For instance, he
was an ardent advocate of the music of Josquin des
Prés, whom he correctly evaluated as the greatest composer of the epoch. He also commended Pierre de la
Rue in warm terms;[5] Ludwig Senfl was another of his
favorite composers. The fact that in 1530 when Luther
wrote his famous letter of praise to Senfl the composer
was a Catholic rather than a Lutheran did not affect
Luther's liking for his music.[6] Luther's attitude appears particularly admirable today, not only because

---

[3] Walter E. Buszin, "Luther on Music," *Musical Quarterly*, XXXII
(Jan., 1946), 80-97.
[4] Paul Nettl, *Luther and Music* (Philadelphia, 1948).
[5] Buszin, *op. cit.*, p. 91.
[6] His high regard for Senfl did not diminish during his later
years. See the *Werke* (Erlangen ed.), LXII, 309.

his musical judgments have stood the rigorous tests of time, but also because he never allowed religious associations to dampen his enthusiasm for excellence in music wherever he found it.

Luther continued to love the music of "the hymns of the papacy," and as late as 1542 sponsored publication of a collection of *Christliche Geseng Lateinisch und Deutsch, zum Begrebnis,* in the preface of which he wrote:

We have chosen songs which are used in the papacy at vigils, masses for the dead, and funerals. Some of these we have printed in this little book and purpose in the future to choose more of them . . . . The songs and notes are precious; it would be a shame and loss were they to disappear; but the texts or words are unchristian.[7]

As far as music was concerned, Luther showed continuous readiness to prove all things, and to hold fast that which is good.

In his preface to the first hymn booklet issued at Wittenberg in 1524, he announced as a reason for using four parts his desire that the young people be trained in music. "Music," he said on another occasion, "is a semi-discipline and task-mistress."[8] Music as Luther viewed the art must be studied rather than merely "enjoyed." Music study, furthermore, must start early, and should form a mandatory part of the school curriculum.

I have always loved music. Those who have mastered this art are made of good stuff, and are fit for any task. It

[7] *Werke,* LVI, 301.
[8] *Ibid.,* LXII, 308.

is necessary indeed that music be taught in the schools. A teacher must be able to sing; otherwise I will not so much as look at him.[9]

From the standpoint of the church musician, Luther's insistence upon music study as a necessary prerequisite to ordination seems especially interesting. "Also, we should not ordain young men into the ministry unless they have become well acquainted with music in the schools."[10] The level of musical competence which Luther's vernacular liturgy, *Deudsche Messe und Ordnung Gottis Diensts*, presupposes in the officiating minister is high. If Luther had intended the *Deudsche Messe* for restricted usage among educated congregations, his musical demands on the officiant might not seem strange, but as he explicitly stated in the preface to his German liturgy, he introduced the vernacular "for the sake of the simple layman."

The officiating minister was required in the *Deudsche Messe* to sing the Epistle in the eighth tone, that is, in the Hypomixolydian mode; the Gospel he was required to sing in the fifth tone, or Lydian mode. Luther himself provided exemplary melodies for both Epistles and Gospels, showing what melodic inflections must be used at first commas, second commas, colons, periods, question marks, and endings of lessons. The melodic formulas for narrative portions of the Gospels differ in Luther's settings from the melodic formulas prescribed for the words of Christ. Christ's words are always to be sung in the lower register of the voice.

[9] *Ibid.*, LXII, 309.
[10] *Ibid.*

Not only the melodic inflections but also the flow of
the rhythm is prescribed in *Deudsche Messe*. Without
here attempting a minute analysis of the music which
Luther wrote for *Deudsche Messe*, we may summarize
by saying that a minister using it would certainly need
to be a vocalist with a considerable range and a well-
developed ability to sight-sing.

Luther himself had a good voice, according to contemporary testimony, and was also a competent lute
player. He dabbled in polyphonic composition, and if
not an adept, at least knew how to write in parts. His
settings for *Deudsche Messe* were assuredly his own
creation. In a famous passage from *Syntagma Musicum*
Johann Walther, Luther's musical assistant who helped
prepare the 1524 *Geystliche Gesangk Buchleyn*, tells
how in 1525 Luther with his aid and that of Conrad
Rupff, singing master at Torgau, set about preparing
the music for the *Deudsche Messe*. "Luther himself
wrote the music for the lessons and the words of insti-
tution. . . . He kept me for three weeks to note down
properly the chants of the Gospels and the Epistles, until the first mass was sung in Wittenberg."[11]

Some conscientious souls eschewed elaborate music in
Luther's day on the same grounds that St. Augustine
had frowned upon it—because it gave too much sensuous
enjoyment. Augustine's attitude had been shared by a
number of prominent religious leaders during the
Middle Ages. Wyclif, Luther's precursor in whittling
down the claims of the papacy, violently inveighed in
his *Sermon on the Contemplative Life* against elaborate

[11] Michael Praetorius, *Syntagma Musicum* (Wittenberg, 1615),
I, 451-452.

music. Luther, however, opposed Augustine's authority with his own in musical matters. "St. Augustine was afflicted with scruples of conscience," Luther said, "but if he were living today, he would hold with us."[12] At another time Luther added:

Next to the word of God, only music deserves being extolled as the mistress and governess of human feelings. . . . Through the medium of music the Holy Spirit placed His gifts in the hands of the Prophets; again through music the devil was driven away, as was the case with Saul, king of Israel. . . . The Fathers and Prophets desired . . . that nothing be more intimately linked up with the Word of God than music.[13]

Consistently, moreover, Luther strove for excellence in evangelical music. Small details such as smudged or incorrectly printed notes in evangelical hymn booklets disturbed him, and he required fresh editions when errors were found in the music. "Luther was always ready to detect misprints and errors in the music. When he did so, he took it away at once, and saw to it that the piece was properly set and rectified."[14]

He was able to understand the peculiar excellencies of the Netherlandish contrapuntists and desired similar standards of artifice in evangelical composition. His description of the beauties of polyphony indicates how sensitive he was to the elaborations of counterpoint:

When natural music is sharpened and polished by art, then one begins to see with amazement the great and perfect wisdom of God in his wonderful work of music, where one

[12] *Werke*, LXII, 111.
[13] *Opera Latina* (Frankfurt, 1873), VII, 552-553.
[14] Nettl, *op. cit.*, p. 61 (quoting Ratzeberger).

voice takes a simple part and around it sing three, four, or five other voices, leaping and springing round about, marvellously gracing the simple part, like a square dance in heaven, with friendly bows, embracings, and hearty swinging of partners.[15]

Because he understood the mission of counterpoint as did no other religious leader of his time, Luther never felt inclined to dispense with trained choirs, without which contrapuntal singing is impossible. His pioneering in hymnody has sometimes been interpreted as a slap at choirs and a friendly pat on congregations. While it is true that he encouraged congregational singing, it is not true that he discouraged trained choirs. As for organ playing, while some scholars such as Schweitzer have thought him not overfriendly to organs, he certainly never showed any animosities. In his exegesis of Psalm 150 he spoke in behalf of organs, and elsewhere he mentioned certain contemporary organists with warm approval.[16] No organs were pulled down in Lutheran areas, as they often were in Zwinglian and Calvinistic areas.

In a purely practical sense, Luther's befriending of church music took the ever-welcome form of financial patronage. Words in themselves would have meant little without the tangible encouragement of money for church music. "The art of music is worthy of being supported and maintained by princes and lords. . . .

[15] R. H. Bainton, *Here I Stand* (New York, 1950), p. 343. Quotation from Luther's foreword to Georg Rhau, *Symphoniae iucundae atque adeo breves quattuor vocum ab optimis pluribusque musicis compositae* (1538).

[16] Karl Anton, *Luther und die Musik* (Zwickau, 1928), contains a useful digest of passages pertaining to instrumental music.

The goods and possessions belonging to monasteries could well be used to take care of these people [the Kantorei],"[17] wrote Luther to John the Steadfast. At a later date he said "Kings, princes, and lords must support music. . . . One reads in the Bible that pious kings supported, maintained, and gave salaries to singers."[18]

In his letter to Senfl, written October 4, 1530, he said, "I love your Bavarian dukes, even though they certainly dislike me. I honor them above all others because they cultivate and honor music."[19] Luther extolled the Catholic Bavarian house simply because the reigning dukes gave liberally in support of a musical establishment. Not by chance was Orlandus Lassus later able to find his most fertile area of enterprise in Munich. The reigning house had already set the pattern of liberal patronage during Luther's lifetime. When during a tour of inspection Luther found music liberally patronized in evangelical Torgau, he praised the town because music was there richly supported: "God Almighty has graciously blessed this city of Torgau," he said after examining its musical establishment. Not by chance was Torgau the place where in 1627, a century after Luther's inspection tour, the first German opera, Schütz's *Dafne*, was presented; a strong musical tradition spanning more than a century had prepared Torgau for this significant milestone of musical progress. Indeed the pre-eminence of German music during the last four centuries can in no small measure be

[17] *Werke*, LIII, 375.
[18] *Werke*, LXII, 308.
[19] See Emil Naumann, *History of Music* (London, 1886), I, 488, n. 1, for comment on the Bavarian dukes as patrons of music.

traced to the numberless little Torgaus where Luther's precepts on music have been taken seriously, for out of the Eisenachs and Halles have come the Bachs and Handels.

In summary, we may say of Luther's musical achievement that he lifted the art to a loftier level than it has attained anywhere else in evangelical thinking. Both theoretically and practically he placed it on a pedestal. No advance we may make in church music will exceed his ideal of what it should be. A practical implementation of his ideals would be today "a consummation devoutly to be wished."

II. REFORMED CHURCH MUSIC

THE BASIC IMPLICATIONS OF CALVINS PHILOSOPHY OF CHURCH MUSIC

I N OUR DAY CALVIN'S PRECEPTS ON church music are more honored in the breach than in the observance. His authority has been invoked for the introduction of certain high-church practices into our large Presbyterian churches;[1] but no responsible scholar has been able to discover evidence in his writings for current practices in the conduct of church music. Modern departures from Calvinist musical theory are basic. These departures from Calvin's straight and narrow path have led modern Presbyterians into an acceptance of instrumental music, and particularly organ music, as a permitted feature of divine worship; into an acceptance of "hymns of human composure" as a permitted feature of divine worship in place of the inspired psalms; into an acceptance of singing in parts as a permitted feature of worship song. But Calvin never allowed organ music in the churches of Geneva. He sanctioned only inspired psalms as material suitable for congregational singing. And he vigorously opposed any

[1] William D. Maxwell, *The Liturgical Portions of the Genevan Service Book* (Edinburgh, 1931), pp. 13, 201-205. On p. 13 the statement is found that Calvin desired weekly communion, that he wished to carry reserved sacrament to the sick, that he desired a declaration of absolution after the confession of sins, that he wanted to retain the open confessional, and also the rite of confirmation.

attempt to introduce part singing into the congregational singing of the psalms.

Calvin, in his sermon on I Samuel, chapter 18, said:

It would be a too ridiculous and inept imitation of papistry to decorate the churches and to believe oneself to be offering God a more noble service in using organs. . . . All that is needed is a simple and pure singing of the divine praises, coming from heart and mouth, and in the vulgar tongue. . . . Instrumental music was tolerated in the time of the Law because the people were then in infancy.[2]

In his commentary on Psalm 92 he pursued the same vein:

In the fourth verse, he [the Psalmist] more immediately addresses the Levites, who were appointed to the office of singers, and calls upon them to employ their instruments of music—not as if this were in itself necessary, only it was useful as an elementary aid to the people of God in these ancient times . . . now that Christ has appeared, and the Church has reached full age, it were only to bury the light of the Gospel, should we introduce the shadows of a departed dispensation. From this, it appears that the Papists, in employing instrumental music, cannot be said so much to imitate the practice of God's ancient people, as to ape it in a senseless and absurd manner, exhibiting a silly delight in that worship of the Old Testament which was figurative, and terminated with the Gospel.[3]

Moreover, after denouncing instrumental music, which he called "a senseless and absurd aping" of figura-

[2] John Calvin, *Homiliae in primum librum Samuelis* (Geneva, 1604), p. 370.
[3] John Calvin, *Commentary on the Book of Psalms* (Edinburgh, 1847), III, 494-495.

tive Old Testament worship, he placed this absolute
restriction on the Calvinist churches: psalms from the
Bible, and psalms only, were to constitute the congregational matter for singing. In his commentary on Psalm
149 he said: "The musical instruments . . . were peculiar
to this infancy of the Church, nor should we foolishly
imitate a practice which was intended only for God's ancient people."[4]   To Psalm 71 he subjoined the following comment:

Musical instruments . . . are banished out of the churches by
the plain command of the Holy Spirit, when Paul, in 1 Cor.
XIV. 13, lays it down as an invariable rule, that we must
praise God, and pray to him only in a known tongue.[5]

In still another passage of like tenor he wrote:

The Levites, under the law, were justified in making use of
instrumental music in the worship of God; it having been
his will to train his people, while they were as yet tender and
like children, by such rudiments, until the coming of Christ.
But now when the clear light of the gospel has dissipated
the shadows of the law, and taught us that God is to be
served in a simpler form, it would be to act a foolish and
mistaken part to imitate that which the prophet enjoined
only upon those of his own time. From this, it is apparent
that the Papists have shown themselves to be very apes in
transferring this to themselves.[6]

The last organ in a Geneva church (a survival from
a Roman monastery) was melted down in order to obtain the tin from the pipes. Two years before the death
of Calvin, at a time when his authority was complete

[4] *Ibid.*, V, 312.
[5] *Ibid.*, III, 98.
[6] *Ibid.*, III, 312.

in Geneva, the minutes of the town council (August 17, 1562) carried the following notice: "It has been thereupon ordained that it shall be melted, that the Hospital shall take what metal it needs, and that the rest shall be kept in pigs."[7]

The tradition concerning the destruction of organs at the hands of the Cromwellian soldiery is by no means our first hint of the antagonism which Calvinist parties in every country vented against organs. In 1567 a tract called *The Praise of Music* carried this notice: "Not so few as one hundred organs were taken down and the pipes sold to make pewter dishes."[8] As early as 1550 Edward VI had issued an injunction (October 26) which indicated an intention of removing organs. In Scotland, according to Peterkin's *Records*, sentiment against organs had so crystallized by 1644 that the General Assembly of that year moved to congratulate the Westminster Assembly because "the organs at Pauls and Peters [Westminster Abbey] have been taken down."[9] Some years earlier in Scotland the "glorious organs of the Chapel Royal were masterfully broken down nor no service used there, but the whole chaplains, choristers and musicians discharged and costly organs altogether destroyed and unuseful."[10] In 1640 in "the

[7] Percy A. Scholes, *The Puritans and Music* (London, 1934), p. 339. Dr. Scholes seeks to exculpate Calvin and the Puritans generally from the oft-repeated charge of animosity to music. He translates the minutes of the Geneva Council in order to prove that the organ pipes were not melted until after considerable attempt over a period of years had been made to sell this organ with an object of turning over the proceeds to the town poor.

[8] *Ibid.*, p. 231.

[9] William McMillan, *The Worship of the Scottish Reformed Church, 1550-1638* (Edinburgh, 1931), p. 99.

[10] *Ibid.*, p. 100.

University of old Aberdeen there stood the remainder of an old organ. . . . This was broken down and complained upon as a thing very intolerable in the church of a college."[11] By 1727 the only church organ in all Scotland was one which stood in the Episcopal church at Aberdeen.[12]

In Massachusetts the leaven implanted by John Cotton, who vigorously denounced organs ("Singing with Instruments was typical, and so a ceremonial worship and therefore is ceased"),[13] and by his successor Cotton Mather ("And because the holy God rejects all He does not command in His worship, He now therefore in effect says to us, I will not hear the melody of thy Organs"),[14] in the year 1711 still so leavened the whole lump of the New England mind that the first organ brought there, though willed by its owner to a Congregational church, was righteously refused. Eventually this famous first organ in New England (owned by Thomas Brattle) found its way into King's Chapel, which at that time was still an Anglican house of worship. The controversy concerning the introduction of organs elicited an intolerable number of pamphlets both in Scotland and New England.[15]

When a project for the introduction of a church organ was placed before Glasgow Presbytery in 1807 it was

[11] *Ibid.*

[12] Sir John Graham Dalyell, *Musical Memoirs of Scotland* (Edinburgh, 1849), p. 131.

[13] John Cotton, *Singing of Psalmes a Gospel-Ordinance* (London, 1647), p. 5.

[14] Cotton Mather, *Magnalia Christi Americana* (London, 1702), Bk. V, p. 55, c. 2.

[15] For a partial list of Scottish pamphlets, see Dalyell, *op. cit.*, p. 137, n. 1.

promptly declared unlawful. So reverentially did the Scottish churches regard Calvin's interpretation of Scripture that authorizations for organs in the various branches of the Presbyterian Church were delayed until 1866 for the Established Church, 1872 for the United Presbyterian Church, and 1883 for the Free Church. And, of course, the ultra-Calvinist Reformed Presbyterian Church of America even now forbids the use of organs and the singing of hymns.

In our own time the *Directory of Worship* for the Presbyterian Church in the United States of America charily skirts the corners of this dangerous topic and leaves unmentioned the whole subject of choirs and organs in chapter iv where it might logically occur.[16] In the 1947 edition of the *Manual of Presbyterian Law* a quotation from the minutes of the General Assembly of 1884 is included, showing a typical handling of a difficult situation. As with so many other vexing problems, the conduct of church music is here thrown back into the arms of each local session.

The Assembly leaves to each Session the delicate and important matter of arranging and conducting the music as to them shall seem most for edification, recommending great caution, prudence, and forbearance in regard to it.[17]

In studying Calvin's attitude toward music we may profitably examine the status of composers in Genevan town life after he gained undisputed control. The com-

[16] *Constitution of the Presbyterian Church in the United States of America* (Philadelphia, 1944), p. 441.
[17] *Manual for Church Officers and Members* (15th ed.; 1947), p. 108.

poser with whom Calvin had most intimate dealings
was Louis Bourgeois.

Historians who wish to give a true philosophical account of
Calvin's influence at Geneva ought probably to refer a great
part of it to the enthusiasm attendant on the pleasure of
singing Bourgeois's melodies.[18]

Although Bourgeois, after flight to Geneva on account
of his Protestant convictions, consumed himself in such
laborious tasks as the instruction of children, he was allowed to languish in poverty during much of his ten-
year sojourn in Geneva.   An account remains showing
his petition for coal and certain other bare necessities of
living.   He was arrested in 1551 and placed in prison
for having changed "without permission" the melodies
of certain of the psalms, which he had himself written
some years earlier.   Robert Bridges (*The Yattendon
Hymnal*) remarks: "He was imprisoned by his em-
ployers for his musical innovations . . . and having
suffered Calvin for sixteen years . . . lost his appointment and left Geneva on account of Calvin's objection
to part-singing."[19]

Douen in his classic work on the Marot Psalter
printed a great many ingenious and inspired polyphonic
settings of tunes from the Genevan Psalter; but none
of these polyphonic settings found its way into the approved public worship of the Calvinist churches.   Innovation or elaboration was not desired by those author-

[18] Winfred Douglas, *Church Music in History and Practice* (New
York, 1937), p. 217.   Douglas takes this statement from Robert
Bridges and H. E. Wooldridge, *The Yattendon Hymnal* (London,
1920), p. 9 ("Notes on the Words and Music").
[19] *The Yattendon Hymnal*, p. 9.

ities who could clap Bourgeois into jail for altering a psalm melody. The crux of the issue lies here: Calvinism denied "the power of the Holy Ghost to inspire men afresh in the Praise of God." Calvin showed literary insight when he set his seal of approval on the psalm-renderings of Clement Marot and Theodore Beza, the two principal authors of the Genevan Psalter.[20] But "there was nothing novel in the mere translating of Psalms into metre.... The adoption of such translations as the *sole* vehicle of congregational sung praise [which] began with John Calvin"[21] was, however, novel.

The dispute over which translations were the most literal, and therefore the most acceptable to God, occupies interminable space in the history of Calvinist churches. "Worship of the Holy Scripture kept the Old Version [Sternhold and Hopkins] in use long after its absurdities were evident to the unprejudiced."[22] In New England the *Bay Psalm Book* appeared in 1640, but the poetry is not considered superior to Sternhold and Hopkins. Rous's version adopted in 1650 by the Scottish General Assembly was disowned by its author on account of the harsh way the Scots accommodated his verse to the "Hebrew original."[23]

As late as the eighteen-eighties there was an organized anti-

[20] Using the Marot-Beza texts and the Guillaume Franc-Louis Bourgeois melodies, the composer Claude Goudimel (1505-1572) constructed admirable polyphonic psalms; but his musical efforts never received any Geneva imprimatur; he later gained a martyr's halo during the St. Bartholomew's massacre.

[21] Douglas, *op. cit.*, p. 219.

[22] *Ibid.*, p. 221.

[23] William D. Maxwell, *An Outline of Christian Worship* (Oxford, 1936), p. 132.

hymn party in the Presbyterian Church in the United States. . . . It issued a monthly journal with eleven editions; these represented pure psalm-singing churches in the United States, the British Isles, and Holland.[24]

Distaste for organs, distaste for hymns, and distaste for part-singing were the typical marks of Calvinist church music. In the *Genevan Service Book of 1556* we find the following rubric for the conduct of the Sunday morning services: "This done [the reciting of a general confession], the people sing a Psalme all together, in a playne tune."[25] William Maxwell comments on this rubric as follows:

The reference to 'playne tune' does not mean only that simple music is to be used, but also that there is to be *no harmony singing*. In the Psalter at the end of the volume [the Genevan Service Book of 1556], the melody line only is given for the various tunes; while Huycke translating and explaining Calvin directs that the Psalm be sung in 'playnesong.'[26]

In Calvin's mind music, when he did allow it, was conceived as Spartan in simplicity; like St. Augustine[27] he knew the emotional power of music sufficiently well to fear it. Douen, a Protestant pastor, a Frenchman, and a scholar whose lifetime was spent in tracing the history of Psalters, said that Calvin, "the pope of Geneva . . . an enemy of all mere pleasure and distraction," was

[24] Scholes, *op. cit.*, p. 253 n. 1.
[25] Maxwell, *The Liturgical Portions of the Genevan Service Book.* (Edinburgh, 1931), p. 88.
[26] *Ibid.*, p. 99.
[27] Augustine, *Confessions*, X, 33.

even an "enemy of music."[28] Whether Calvin personally liked or disliked music is beside the point. He certainly conceded its power; but as he pointed out in a
passage on Job, music could be blameworthy, and most
commonly men turn the flute and tabor and similar
things to "bad ends."[29]

However explicit he may have been, obviously most
Presbyterian churches today are not prepared to accept
his musical philosophy. Instead they turn to doctrinal
expressions in music which are alien and even hostile to
Reformed teaching. Leading Presbyterian churches
have, for instance been known to advertise performances
of the Verdi *Requiem,* of Mozart masses, of the Fauré
Requiem, of the Palestrina *Stabat Mater,* and of similar
works. Because they are included in their worship services, authorization is inevitably implied.

Cardinal Sadolet is now enjoying the sweetest vindi-
cation of all of Calvin's opponents. He has seen Calvin's spiritual progeny discard the fundamental prin-

[28] Orentin Douen, *Clément Marot et le Psautier Huguenot* (Paris,
1878-1879), I, 377.
[29] John Calvin, *Sermons upon the Booke of Job,* chap. 21. As
translated by Arthur Golding (1574), pp. 373-74, the passage reads:
"The Flute and the Taber, & such other like things are. . . to be
condemned. . . in respect of mens abusing of them. . . .For certainly
the Taber doth no sooner sound to make men merrie, but there is
always lightly some vanitie, I say not superfluous but beastly. . . .
Musike of itself cannot be condemned: but forasmuch as the worlde
doth almost alwayes abuse it, we ought to bee so much the more
circumspect. . . .Wee see at this day that they which use musike doo
swell with poyson against God, they become hardharted, they will
have their songs, . . .full of villane and ribauldrie. And after-
warde they fall to dauncing, which is the chiefest mischiefe of all
. . . . The spirit of God condemneth . . . the vanities that are committed in musike, . . . bycause that men delight too much in them: and
when they set their delight and pleasure in these base and earthly
things, they thinke not a whit upon God."

ciples of Calvinist musical reform. Calvin cannot be
made to say the same thing as Sadolet (though some un-
easy Calvinists would now have him do so) merely because he wrote a letter June 10, 1543, in which he said
"music is either the first or one of the principal" means
of "recreating man and giving him pleasure."[30] The
point is: though he conceded the emotional power of
music he excluded from divine worship organs, polyphony, and all songs except psalms. Without these
music, as presently conceived, scarcely can be said to
exist.

[30] Charles Garside, "Calvin's Preface to the Psalter: A Re-Appraisal," *Musical Quarterly*, XXXVII (Oct., 1951), 570.

III. JOHN MERBECKE
AND THE FIRST ENGLISH
PRAYER BOOK

THE FIRST ENGLISH PRAYER BOOK
was issued in 1549. This first prayer book, unlike its 1552 and 1559 successors, was immediately followed by the publication of *The Booke of Common Praier noted* in which was "conteyned so muche of
the Order of Common Prayer as is to be song in
Churches."[1]

The central figure in the compilation of the first
prayer book, was (as is commonly known) Archbishop
Cranmer. Not so well known, however, as was his part
in the compilation of the prayer book, but still worth
noting, was his responsibility for the musical style of the
companion volume. The rubrics of the prayer book of
1549 (unlike the rubrics contained in later editions of
The Book of Common Prayer) specifically enjoined the
singing of certain portions of the service. The Athanasian Creed (known as the *Quicunque vult*) "shall be
sung (or said),"[2] and, "to the end the people may the
better hear in such places where they do sing, there shall
the lessons be sung in a *playne tune* after the manner of
distinct reading: and likewise the Epistle and Gospel."[3]

[1] John Merbecke, *The Booke of Common Praier noted* (London,
1550). These words occur in the preface. See Francis Procter and
W. H. Frere, *A New History of The Book of Common Prayer*
(London, 1901), p. 65.
[2] *The First Prayer Book of King Edward the Sixth* (1549; reprinted in facsimile, London, 1844), folio v verso.
[3] *Ibid.*, folio i verso.

The rubrics requiring that certain portions be sung in
a "playne tune" meant, of course, that the priest and his
choir were to sing the type of unaccompanied unisonous
melodies already in traditional use in the old church.

English composers during the Middle Ages had pioneered in the development of polyphony, but Cranmer,
to whom "the decisive change which had been given
to the character of the Reformation under Edward VI
was wholly due," advocated for one reason or another
"the banishment of figured music from the Church."[4]
As early as 1544 (three years before Edward acceded
to the throne) Cranmer had made his first translation
of a liturgical Latin function into the English language.
His *Litany* of 1544 was sung in plainsong—the same
type of unisonous melody he wanted used in the sung
portions of the first prayer book, adopted five years
later.[5] Cranmer explained to Henry VIII the method
which he had used in adapting plainsong melodies to
English words in a famous letter: "I have travail'd to
make the verses in English and have put the *Latin note*
unto the same."[6] The notes for the original Latin
words were thus adapted to, rather than newly composed for, Cranmer's English translation. There were,
of course, in musical notation many alternate traditional
melodies for the same sets of Latin words; Cranmer's
task therefore included also the task of selecting melo-

[4] "Figured music" here means polyphonic music. See Edward F.
Rimbault, *John Merbecke's Book of Common Prayer as used in the
Chapel Royal of Edward VI* (London, 1845), p. xiii.

[5] Winfred Douglas, *Church Music in History and Practice* (New
York, 1937), pp. 79-80.

[6] William Maskell, *Monumenta Ritualia Ecclesiae Anglicanae*
(2nd ed.; Oxford, 1882), I, cxii. Maskell modernized the spelling.

dies as well as pointing words. He inevitably chose the simplest melodies. His reason for choosing simple plainsong melodies was expressed in his statement: "In mine opinion, the song that shall be made would not be full of notes, but as near as may be, for every syllable a note; so that it may be sung distinctly and devoutly."[7]

Cranmer wanted plainsong adapted to English words, and he furthermore wanted simple plainsong melodies of a syllabic type—melodies with a note for every syllable. He naturally selected a composer who would be a willing instrument of his musical policy when it was decided to push through the press a musical counterpart of the prayer book. John Merbecke, the man whom he chose for the task of adapting and composing the music for *The Booke of Common Praier noted* ("noted" means, of course, set in musical notation) has been dubbed Cranmer's "obedient tool."[8] Cranmer, not a singer himself, labored under the delusion that the easiest melody to sing is one with only one musical note to a syllable.

As not infrequently happens when the reverend clergy dictate musical rules without skilled musical advice, the Archbishop's excellent intention of making the services easy for congregations to sing and understand was largely defeated by a faulty method: for music of the syllabic type is far harder to sing well than that of a more flowing movement, in which several notes often occur to a single syllable.[9]

Cranmer had, however, his own way with the music

[7] *Ibid.*
[8] H. E. Wooldridge, *Oxford History of Music,* Vol. 2: *1400-c. 1600* (London, 1932), p. 243.
[9] Winfred Douglas, *op. cit.,* pp. 80-81.

edition of the first prayer book, and fortunately the composer who accomplished the actual work was artist enough to complete the music edition in a creditable manner, even under the strait-jacketing of the one-note-to-a-syllable idea. But *The Prayer Book Dictionary*, commenting on the necessary revisions and curtailments that Merbecke made in suiting the plainsong of the Latin repertory to the translated English words, summarizes thus: "Nothing but a yearning for directness, such as would enforce rather than obscure the sense of the text, could have justified Merbecke's revisions of the traditional melodies."[10] The same idea is borne out in the words of another authority on Merbecke's musical prayer book: "The old Gregorian melodies were reduced to their simplest musical expression; all melodic flourishes were cut off, so that nothing would remain but pure musical declamation."[11]

Even after making these adjustments, however, Merbecke's musical prayer book did not completely satisfy those reforming spirits abroad who wished to sweep the field entirely clean and therefore rejected any plain song as a Romish heritage.[12] Of the first prayer book it was said by Hooper in a letter to Bullinger, "The mass priests, although they are compelled to discontinue the use of the Latin language, yet carefully observe the same tone and manner of chanting to which they were heretofore accustomed in the papacy."[13] In every way

[10] George Harford and Morley Stevenson, *The Prayer Book Dictionary* (London, 1925), p. 589.

[11] James Moffatt (ed.), *Handbook to the Church Hymnary* (London, 1927), p. 429.

[12] Procter and Frere, *op. cit.*, p. 66.

[13] *Ibid.*, p. 68.

the first prayer book and its musical counterpart written by Merbecke did not go far enough to please the radical party.[14]

Merbecke in referring to the Holy Communion used the term "Mass" in his 1550 music edition. The Agnus Dei was included; the Gloria came immediately after the Kyrie, and prayers for the dead were set to music. In all these details he simply followed the first prayer book. When Parliament, however, authorized the second prayer book of 1552, into which was inserted the so-called "Black Rubric,"[15] several deletions were simultaneously enacted, among which were the rubrics enjoining a choral service. At a stroke Merbecke's labors lost their relevance to prayer-book worship. During the next century scholars who knew of his work disparaged it, not only because it retained an affinity to Gregorian music, but more emphatically because the words which he set to music were in several cases (certainly through no fault of his) offensive to "enlightened" Protestant conscience of later times. The voluminous Strype, for instance, dismissed Merbecke contemptuously because in his musical setting "[sung] prayer is made for the deceased and the soul departed is held to be in a middle state till the last judgment."[16]

Not until Tractarian times did *The Booke of Com-*

[14] Martin Bucer complained: "In many of your churches there is still found a studied representation of the execrated Mass in vestures, lights, washing of the cup, carrying the book from right to left of the table, having the table where the altar was, lifting the paten and cup..." (Procter and Frere, *op. cit.*, p. 68).

[15] Declaring against "any real and essential presence" in the Sacrament.

[16] John Strype, *Ecclesiastical Memorials* (Oxford, 1822), II, 1, 418.

mon Praier noted regain the favor which it had enjoyed for such a brief time after its initial publication. But with the revival of liturgical interest Merbecke again came into vogue because "it appears incontrovertible that the English Liturgy and its suggested music were formulated together, and the *sung service* set forth as the standard worship of the Church as a whole."[17] His "noted booke" then began to make its way so amazingly as to become the music of the Eucharist at the opening of Lambeth Conferences.[18] And now of course, "it is officially set forth by the Episcopal Church in America."[19] Since at present it not only appears that the musical reputation of Merbecke will continue to grow but that his most widely known work, the plainsong setting of the sung Eucharist, will continue to receive ever wider usage (at least in Anglican circles), a study of his life history seems here apposite.

He was a pioneer in several fields. In 1550 he published contemporaneously with *The Booke of Common Praier noted* another important work, the first concordance to the entire English Bible.[20] His musical genius, in the perhaps overenthusiastic words of Sir Richard Terry, merits him "a place among the musical Olympians to whom we tender our deepest admiration, and offer our sincerest homage and reverence."[21] But since his achievements in addition to the composition of music

[17] Douglas, *op. cit.*, p. 82.

[18] *Ibid.*, p. 87.

[19] *The Hymnal of the Protestant Episcopal Church* (New York, 1940), p. 743.

[20] E. H. Fellowes *et al.* (eds.), *Tudor Church Music* (London, 1929), X, 159.

[21] R. R. Terry, in *Proceedings of the Musical Association, Forty-Fifth Session, 1918-1919* (Leeds, 1920), p. 94.

included the compilation of an epoch-making concordance, the writing of several theological treatises, and
even the writing of some poetry, his reputation does not
stand or fall on his musical accomplishment alone.

His early life is still obscure. The famous musical
historian, Charles Burney, said he was born in 1523;[22]
subsequent research has revealed, however, the birth of
a son to John Merbecke in the year 1536.[23] Since it
seems hardly likely that he exhibited his precocity in be-
coming a father at the early age of thirteen, the 1523
date, one which a number of historians have accepted,
needs revision. The date of his birth may now be tenta-
tively placed in the second year of Henry VIII's
reign.[24]

If his beginnings are obscure, one episode in his early
life of a thoroughly dramatic kind is well enough documented. In 1539, annoyed at the proliferation of un-
regulated Protestant sentiment, Henry VIII issued his
"Act Abolishing Diversity in Opinions" which became
popularly known as the "Whip with Six Strings."[25] In
order to enforce the Six Articles, ecclesiastical commissions were empowered to sit quarterly in each diocese
with the purpose of inquiring after the spread of heresy.
Merbecke at the time of the Six Articles held a position
as organist in St. George's Chapel at Windsor, and
with three associates had become inflamed with a zeal

[22] *Ibid.*, p. 76. Charles Burney, *A General History of Music*
(London, 1776-1789); Vols. II and III mention Merbecke. I myself, despite Sir Richard's explicit statement, think it likely he got
his birthdate from some other source than Burney.
[23] *Tudor Church Music*, X, 155.
[24] *Ibid.*
[25] James Gairdner, *The English Church in the Sixteenth Century*
(London, 1902), p. 207.

for Scriptural studies. As he himself confessed, he had
"in a maner never tasted the swetnes of learned letters,"
having been brought up at Windsor "in the study of
Musike and plaiyng on Organs, wherin I consumed vainly the greatest part of my life";[26] but about the time of
the Six Articles he had turned much of his energy into
theological channels. Shortly after their promulgation
he fell into the clutches of the law. In his house, which
was searched under writ from the King on March 18,
1543,[27] were discovered damaging pieces of evidence,
among them his half-completed concordance. Inspired
by the reading of a complete Bible with notes (Thomas
Matthews' edition) Merbecke, as he told his judges
when he later came to trial under the Six Articles, had
set about copying the whole of it by hand. He did this,
he said, because he was too poor to afford the purchase
of his own Bible. A friend of his named Turner had
however suggested to him, he told his judges, the more
fruitful idea of making a concordance, rather than the
wasting of time in mere hand-copying of the Bible.[28]

Joyfully accepting his friend Turner's suggestion,
Merbecke immediately set to work. But when the
search of his house was undertaken not only was the
half-finished concordance found but also in his own
handwriting a copy of an epistle of that "greate Clerke
Master Jhon Calvin, written against the same sixe
articles."[29] Calvin had declared:

[26] *Tudor Church Music*, X, 159 (Preface to 1550 *Concordance*,
a. ij.).
[27] *Domestic State Papers of Henry VIII*, XVIII, pt. 1, 164 (292).
[28] Sir John Hawkins, *A General History of the Science and
Practice of Music* (London, 1853), I, 449.
[29] *Tudor Church Music*, X, 159.

The holly masse when the priest doth consecrate the body
of our Lord is pollutyd difformyd sinfull and open robery
of the glory of God from the which a Christian harte ought
both to abhore and flee: and the eleevacion of the sacrament
is the symylitude of the setting up of Images of the calves in
the temple buylded by Jeroboam and that is more abomina-
cion than the Sacrifices done by the Jewes in Jeroboams
temple to those calves; and certayne and sure it is that Christ
himselfe is made in this masse mens laughinge stocke.[30]

Merbecke's doom seemed therefore sealed. He says
tersely that he was "taken in the labirinth and trouble-
some net of a lawe called the Statute of vi articles, where
by the meanes of good woorkers for my dispatche, I was
quickly condempned and Judged to death."[31]

But John Foxe, the martyrologist, adds other details.
The "good woorkers" for his dispatch were certain en-
vious musicians appointed to work alongside him at St.
George's chapel. These "good woorkers" also produced
information against Anthony Person, a priest, Robert
Testwood, a "singing man," and Henry Filmer, a tailor
practising his trade at Windsor. Person in the hearing
of others had declared that the elevation of the Host
in the Mass was a worse desecration than the hanging of
Christ between two thieves.[32] Testwood had dissuaded
people from making pilgrimages, "and had stricken off
with a key the nose of an alabaster image of the Virgin
Mary which stood behind the high altar of St. George's
Chapel."[33] The informer against Testwood was Robert

[30] *Ibid.*, X, 158.
[31] *Ibid.*, X, 159 (quoted from Merbecke's preface to the 1550
Concordance).
[32] James Gairdner, *op. cit.*, p. 227.
[33] John Foxe, *Actes and Monuments* (London, 1583), p. 1212,
c. 2.

Phillips,[34] a singer who "gloried in himself."[35] ("Whensoever Phillips came the longest song with the most verses in it would be set up for him.")[36] Testwood according to his singing rival, had responded one day to the words "O redemptrix et salvatrix" in salutation of the Virgin with the words *"non* redemptrix *nec* salvatrix."[37] (Phillips, ironically, lived to see the rewards of his self-aggrandizement, later enjoying appointments in the chapel establishments of both Edward and Mary.[38])

The fourth figure in the Windsor heresy trial was Filmer, a tailor. He was sentenced to death because he had made the statement that if Christ existed corporeally in the sacrament of the altar, he, Filmer, had then eaten twenty gods in his lifetime.[39] The trial took place, July 26, 1543, some four months after the first searches were made. The next day Person, Testwood, and Filmer were burned at the stake.[40] The spot of their execution was later called "the Chapter Garden."[41] Their style of execution called for a "ripping up of the men in each other's presence, a tearing

[34] Merbecke was primarily an organist rather than a chorister.

[35] Hawkins, *op. cit.*, I, 450.

[36] *Ibid.*, p. 450 (quoted from John Foxe's *Acts and Monuments*).

[37] Singers in the later Middle Ages took greater liberties with the text than this comparatively innocuous instance might suggest. The Tridentine fathers condemned farsed Kyries and Tropes, which had degenerated into occasions for nonsense and even obscenity.

[38] If Phillips had survived into Elizabeth's reign, he would have been completely at home in her Chapel Royal Establishment. See R. R. Terry, *The Music of the Roman Rite* (London, 1931), p. 217, on the religious indifferentism that prevailed in her chapel establishment.

[39] Gairdner, *op. cit.*, p. 227.

[40] Several notorious burnings under the Six Articles Act had already occurred at Smithfield (Barnes, Garret, and Jerome).

[41] *Tudor Church Music*, X, 158.

off of the arms, and the rubbing of their hearts upon their mouths and faces."[42]

Merbecke escaped this. Certainly his offenses were not less than those of the others. The evidence against him was in writing, and the evidence against the other three was merely hearsay. So overwhelming was the case against him that John Foxe indeed thought he had been executed with the others at Windsor on July 27, 1543.[43] Later, howver, he made the correction: "Merbecke is not dead, God be praised, and yet to the present singeth merrily, and playeth on the organs."[44] Foxe, however, when he made his correction[45] did not attempt to explain why Merbecke alone escaped death. Though he was married and the father of a seven-year-old child, his family responsibilities probably had no bearing on his reprieve; during the tiresome months of his confinement in Marshalsea prison his wife is known to have experienced the greatest difficulty seeing him.[46] Stephen Gardiner, bishop of Winchester, certainly did not help secure his ultimate pardon[47] merely because Merbecke was a man with family. Gardiner did have the healthiest respect for the "noble art of music," however, and since Merbecke had already mastered this art to perfection, his talent (as the further record of the case given below shows) aroused Gardiner's interest. Edward Hall, chronicler of *The Triumphant Reigne of Henry VIII*, remarked that Merbecke's "honestie and innocen-

[42] Gairdner, *op. cit.*, p. 157.
[43] J. Eric Hunt, *Cranmer's First Litany, 1544, and Merbecke's Book of Common Prayer Noted, 1550* (London, 1939), p. 33.
[44] Hawkins, *op. cit.*, I, 450.
[45] Hunt, *op. cit.*, p. 33.
[46] *Tudor Church Music*, X, 158.
[47] *Ibid.*

cie purchased hym the kynges Pardon,"[48] but Gardiner was the intermediary.

First apprehended during March of 1543, Merbecke was not finally reprieved until some two months after the execution of his three colleagues in heresy. The execution occurred at the end of July; the reprieve was granted Merbecke, through Gardiner's influence at Court, on October 4 of the same year.[49] Chronicler Hall may have meant by "honestie and innocencie" that Merbecke retracted and recanted; Gardiner undoubtedly wanted Merbecke to capitulate and to recant.[50] And Merbecke did go so far as to offer in his defense the statement that he had copied Calvin's diatribe against the Mass before the Six Articles were themselves promulgated for the guidance of harassed English conscience. Furthermore, in order to show his method in compiling the offending concordance, which was complete through the letter "L" at the time of Merbecke's seizure, he offered to extract for the edification of the trial commissioners the Scripture locations for words beginning with the letter "M."[51]

In a day's time working with the aid of a Latin concordance Merbecke extracted enough Scripture locations to fill three sheets of paper. His method for a word such as "man" would be as follows: he would take the Latin equivalent, in this case, "homo," and find every

[48] Edward Hall, *The Triumphant Reigne of Henry VIII* (London, 1904), II, 344.

[49] *Domestic State Papers of Henry VIII*, XVIII, pt. 2, 145 (247).

[50] Henry had already pardoned great numbers who had recanted. The first five hundred persons indicted at London under the Six Articles Act were pardoned (T. M. Lindsay, *History of the Reformation* [New York, 1928], p. 348).

[51] Hawkins, *op. cit.*, I, 450.

reference in the Latin Concordance to Scripture using
the word "homo"; he would then immediately look up
the passage not in the Vulgate but in the English Bible,
writing down the complete sentence in which the translated expression "man" occurred. Dr. Oking, one of
the ecclesiastical commissioners sitting on the case, so
admired Merbecke's aptness and industry as to remark
freely that Merbecke "had been better employed than
his accusers."[52]

Gardiner also suggested to Merbecke that he save
himself by offering names of other heretics. But the
record shows that Merbecke refused to buy his pardon
with the lives of his associates. At his third examination
before Bishop Gardiner in the latter's house at Southwark Merbecke found the Bishop with a roll in his
hand awaiting his entrance into the hall. Going toward
the window Gardiner called to him: "Merbecke, wilt
thou cast awaye thyself?" "No," replied Merbecke.
"Yes, thou goest about it, for thou wilt utter nothing.
What a devill made thee to meddle with the Scriptures?
Thy vocation was another way wherein thou hast
a goodly gyft if thou didst esteem it." "Yes," replied
Merbecke, "I do esteem it, and have done my part
therin accordyng to that little knowledge God hath
geven me." "And why the devill dydst thou not hold
thee there?" Merbecke then replied that he felt that
the making of a concordance was a work well pleasing to
Divine Will. Gardiner's parting thrust was: "I do not
discommend thy dilligence, but why shuldest thou

[52] *Ibid.*, I, 449. Foxe, *op. cit.*, p. 1217, c. 2, attributed this remark, however, to Henry VIII rather than Dr. Oking.

meddle with that thing that pertayned not to thee?"[53]

Gardiner's experience with Scripture parrots, as he called them,[54] gave him an early and permanent dislike for all "contumacious Bible students." But Merbecke, although a fervent student of Scripture, knew how to give the soft answer that turneth away wrath. More than one student of his career has praised him for his utter candor and sincerity;[55] his sincerity was, however, coupled with meekness.

Obviously his "goodly gift" in Bishop Gardiner's estimation was his musical talent; Henry VIII, who pardoned him, was probably influenced by his "gift" also. England's most musical monarch, he was one of the two British kings who have themselves composed.[56] Several musical settings of the mass survive from Henry's youthful years, and one of his anthems, accepted by historians as genuine, is still occasionally heard in English churches. He played the lute, the organ, and the harpsichord; English court life naturally reflected his tastes.[57] If it cannot be proved that he pardoned Merbecke because he appreciated the latter's musical talent, it is at least known that he regretted the death of Testwood, the heretic who was a "singing man."[58]

[53] Foxe, *op. cit.*, p. 1215.

[54] Gairdner, *op. cit.*, p. 235.

[55] R. R. Terry, "Forgotten Composers," *Musical News*, LXVIII (no. 1718), 202, 227.

[56] Concerning the musical achievements of Henry V, "mirror of Christian kings," see Manfred Bukofzer's "The Music of the Old Hall Manuscript," *Musical Quarterly*, XXXV (Jan., 1949), 57-59.

[57] S. L. Ollard, *A Dictionary of English Church History* (London, 1919), p. 260.

[58] See Hawkins, *op. cit.*, p. 450.

The bulk of Merbecke's polyphonic music had obviously been composed some considerable time before the date of his trial. It is certain he had written a large amount of Latin music,[59] even though surviving "the havoc wrought with liturgical works, when important libraries such as that of Eton College were despoiled, and when Oxford University Library disappeared altogether,"[60] only three of Merbecke's polyphonic compositions with Latin text remain today. One of these works is a mass and the other two are motets. In addition to the three Latin polyphonic works, there is a three-part carol in honor of the Virgin.[61]

Later in life, after Merbecke abandoned the composition of music and turned to the writing of polemical works such as *The Ripping Up of the Pope's Fardel*, he undoubtedly learned to regret his time spent writing carols, masses, motets, and the like. Percy Scholes, who calls Merbecke "a Puritan of the earlier period of English Puritanism," after commenting on the enormous number of passages of a polemical nature Merbecke extracted for his *Book of Commonplaces*, states that "no doubt this kind of activity at last came to hinder his musical composition."[62] Not only was his creative activity hindered during his later years, but also it seems unlikely that Merbecke can have done much performing on organs after 1550, for in that year by a

[59] R. R. Terry, in *Proceedings of the Musical Association*, 1918-1919, p. 88.
[60] R. R. Terry, *The Music of the Roman Rite* (quotation), p. 218.
[61] Hawkins is the only source for this carol.
[62] Percy A. Scholes, *The Puritans and Music* (London, 1934), p. 302.

decree of Edward VI organ playing was abolished in
the Windsor Chapel. However, the decree had it that
he and another organist at Windsor were to "enjoy their
several fees during their lives if they continue at
Windsor in as large and ample a manner as if organ
playing had continued in the Church."[63] In that year
even the great organ at St. Paul's "was finally dev-
astated and silenced," the choir disbanded, and the
clergy reduced to bare surplices.[64]

Merbecke, who inveighed against all use of instruments in his later publications, wrote in typical vein
when he said: "To sing with instruments was a part of
the Ceremonial service of the Temple, which doth no
more pertain to us than the Sacrifices, Censings, and
Lights."[65]   With the continued stipend from St.
George's, and a possible partial loss of hearing,[66] Merbecke settled down in old age to the compilation of a
two-thousand-odd-page encyclopedia of Reformed doctrine, the so-called *Book of Commonplaces;* his death
year has been placed at 1585, one year after the publication of his last book, appropriately entitled *A Dialogue
between Youth and Age.*

The prominent musicians of the sixteenth century in
England who renounced their allegiance to Rome were
Taverner, Tye, and Merbecke.[67] Taverner, Tye, and
Merbecke also were the three composers who gave up
the serious practice of the musical art at the very peak

[63] *Tudor Church Music,* X, 156.
[64] Procter and Frere, *op. cit.,* p. 85.
[65] John Merbecke, *A Booke of Notes and Commonplaces, with
Their Expositions* (London, 1581), p. 543.
[66] R. R. Terry, in *Proceedings,* p. 85.
[67] R. R. Terry, *The Music of the Roman Rite,* p. 217.

of their powers.[68]   Taverner accepted employment as
an agent of Thomas Cromwell; Tye spent his last sixteen years ministering as an Anglican parson; Merbecke
spent his declining years buttressing Reformed theology.

Their music, which they came to distrust, has, on the
other hand, saved them from oblivion. "The fame of
John Merbecke is at its height today, nearly four
hundred years after the publication of his *Book of Common Prayer noted.*"[69]   Late in life Merbecke found
more pleasure in "touching also the Luciferous pride
of that monstrous Dragon of Rome, tickling him about
the mouth to awake him out of his deadly errors, wherein he hath snorted so long,"[70] than in the practice of
music; but his musical talent saved him from the stake
and conjoined his name to the historic enterprise of
1549, the first prayer book.

Though he spent his last twenty-five years wandering over the desert sands in the dark world and wide of
polemical controversy while that one talent which is
death to hide was lodged with him useless, he had already accomplished enough day-labor before the light of
his musical talent was extinguished to save his name
forever from oblivion.

[68] Terry in *Proceedings*, p. 94, conjectures that Merbecke gave up
music because of "conscientious scruples."
[69] Hunt, *op. cit.*, p. v.
[70] Terry in *Proceedings*, p. 87; quoted from Merbecke's *Conference between the Pope and his Secretary* (1582).

IV. BACH'S RELIGIOUS ENVIRONMENT

THE WELLSPRINGS OF RELIGIOUS EMOTION THAT NOURISHED HIS CREATIVE LIFE

TO SUCH MONUMENTAL PROPORtions has grown J. S. Bach's stature in the world of music today that "we may safely judge a person's understanding of music by his attitude toward Bach."[1] In our own generation his dominance is everywhere so complete that he is the "guide of musicians the world over,"[2] and everywhere, gladly acknowledging his pre-eminence, "musicians see in him their greatest teacher, the master who sets the standard in essential matters of composition, the sure guide who shows the right way."[3]

Alfred Einstein contends that Bach was "a great river into which all things flowed, and all that his own age and the ages before him had done and dreamed of were his tributaries."[4] So amazing was the "superhuman mastery," the "faultless perfection," of his art, that modern historians have often found it difficult to account for his "artistic omnipotence" in prosaic human terms.[5]

[1] Hugo Leichtentritt, *Music, History, and Ideas* (Cambridge, 1940), p. 159.
[2] Henry Prunières, *A New History of Music* (New York, 1943), p. 341.
[3] Leichtentritt, *op. cit.*, p. 158.
[4] Alfred Einstein, *A Short History of Music* (New York, 1947), p. 131.
[5] Cecil Gray, *The History of Music* (New York, 1931), p. 158.

But if today he is universally admired, certainly during his own day he was placed on no such unique pedestal as he now occupies two centuries after his death. During his lifetime he won only local recognition as a musical composer. A contemporary said of his compositions: "Turgidity has led [him] from the natural to the artificial, and from the lofty to the somber."[6] And in the same vein: "One admires the onerous labor and uncommon effort—which, however, are vainly employed. ..."[7] The post as director of the music for the churches of Leipzig which he occupied during the last quarter century of his life did not seek him, and in fact he was only a poor third choice after more famous men, Telemann and Graupner (whose names are now largely forgotten) had been approached, but had declined the post. As one town councilor expressed himself before Bach was chosen for the Leipzig cantorate: "Since the best man could not be obtained, mediocre ones would have to be accepted."[8]

More than a year before his death, the Leipzig Council, with scant consideration for Bach's personal feelings, already had set afoot plans for the choice of his successor, "in case the Capellmeister and Cantor Mr. Sebastian Bach should die."[9] Had Bach been in such a state of health during 1749 that he was unable to perform his duties, the search for his successor might have been justi-

[6] J. A. Scheibe, *Critischer Musikus* (Leipzig, 1745), p. 63 (translated in H. T. David and A. Mendel, *The Bach Reader* [New York, 1945], p. 238).

[7] Scheibe, *op. cit.*, p. 63 (David and Mendel, p. 238).

[8] *Excerpts from the Proceedings of the Town Council of Leipzig,* in David and Mendel, p. 88.

[9] David and Mendel, *op. cit.*, p. 185.

fiable; but the record of his composition, especially his work on *The Art of Fugue,* shows how active and immensely industrious he continued to be until almost the hour of death. (His death on July 28, 1750, came as the result of postoperative complications; a traveling English oculist operated on Bach's eyes and later wrote: "Despite having all circumstances in his favor, motions of the pupil, light, etc., . . . upon drawing the curtain we found the bottom defective."[10]) When he died no encomiums were read over him in the churches he had served; he was remembered with no gracious minute of appreciation from the Leipzig town council; no memorial was erected over his grave; and in time the very location of the burial spot was forgotten.

Because then in large measure his true stature seems to have gone unappreciated in the churches he served during his lifetime, it is now sometimes assumed that he was the victim of a church system in which orthodoxy was enshrined, while creativity was closely cabined, cribbed, and confined. The friction between Bach and his pastor at Mülhausen, between Bach and the subdeacon at Nicholas Church in Leipzig, and especially the friction between Bach and the rector of St. Thomas School where the choirboys were trained have provided certain musical historians with the examples they have needed to prove their thesis: Bach was crushed by the decadent church life of his day and age.

Associated with this thesis has been the idea that had Bach only enjoyed the fresh air of a more liberal church system and had he only escaped the stifling closeness of rigid orthodoxy, his whole professional life would have

[10] C. S. Terry, *Bach: A Biography* (London, 1933), p. 263.

been altered for the better. But had the cobwebs
around him been swept away, as some modern historians not overfond of rigid orthodoxy like to conceive
the matter; had Bach lived under an "unfettered"
church system; had the mass of petty restrictions that
overbore him, for instance, at Leipzig,[11] been removed:
would he then indeed have found a more congenial at-
mosphere in which to develop his creative talents, a
better climate in which to grow artistically?

Bach did at least find in the eighteenth-century
Lutheran milieu the most important thing a sacred composer needs: the vital stimulus to compose new church
music constantly. True, his impulse to create new sacred masterpieces on a grand scale abated after 1735;
but, as we shall later see, the decline in productivity of
church works during the last fifteen years of his life did
not come about as the result so much of a change in
the official policy of the Leipzig churches toward new
music as the result of a personal rift between Bach and
the head of St. Thomas School. Our thesis runs thus:
Bach found in Lutheran churches, and in Lutheran
churches only, an opportunity to present his new music
week after week before receptive and intelligent audiences. During one comparatively brief period when he
did absent himself from a high Lutheran environment,
(1717 until 1723) he worked for a Calvinist prince, Leopold of Anhalt-Cöthen. Significantly enough at Cöthen
he wrote no *St. Matthew Passion*, no *Christmas Oratorio*, no five-year cycle of church cantatas. Prince Leopold,
because he was a Calvinist, felt obliged to frown on any

[11] Philipp Spitta, *Johann Sebastian Bach* (London, 1899), II, 191-
193.

other type of church music than the unadorned psalms in meter.[12] Bach found only in high Lutheran orthodoxy a congenial environment in which to produce the two Passions, the *Magnificat*, and the so-called "oratorios."

Luther, as was seen in chapter i, had set a favorable pattern for church music when he placed music next to theology in his scale of religious values. The devil, he said, "takes flight at the sound of music, just as he does at the words of theology, and for this reason the prophets always combined theology and music, the teaching of truth and the chanting of psalms and hymns."[13] His high esteem for elaborate figural music led him, as we have seen, to commission such an eminent polyphonist as the Roman Catholic Ludwig Senfl to write Latin motets (founded upon Gregorian melodies) for his spiritual delectation.[14] It was Luther, the writer of such hymns as *Ein' Feste Burg* and *Vom Himmel Hoch*, the champion of underpaid musicians, the performer on a musical instrument himself, who had established a favorable climate (in those churches which subscribed to his teaching) for the flowering of music such as Bach's.

Despite, then, the allurements the title bestowed on him by the Calvinist Prince Leopold of Anhalt-Cöthen exercised (and he admitted he waited for several months before making up his mind finally to move away

---

[12] Terry, *op. cit.*, p. 116.

[13] F. A. Beck, *Dr. M. Luthers Gedanken über die Musik* (Berlin, 1825), p. 58 (translated in H. Grisar, *Luther* [London, 1918], II, 171).

[14] Grisar, *op. cit.*, II, 171; see also *Dr. Martin Luthers sämmtliche Werke* (Erlangen, 1854), LX, 60.

from Cöthen, because "it did not seem at all proper for me to change my position of Capellmeister for Cantor"),[15] Bach did at last decide he must again obtain a post as director of music in a Lutheran environment in order to fulfil his self-appointed mission. It was no mere impulse which caused him to move away from Calvinist Cöthen to Lutheran Leipzig; we now know that he struggled with the intricate doctrinal differences which separated Calvinists from Lutherans in the early eighteenth century; at Cöthen he fortified himself by reading Luther's seven-volume collected works in the 1539 edition (this collection was the most expensive item in the large theological library he left at his death in 1750).[16] At Cöthen, also, he read polemical blasts against Calvinism written by a learned seventeenth-century professor of theology at Leipzig University, Dr. August Pfeiffer, whose *Anticalvinismus*[17] helped to sustain him. At Cöthen, moreover, he placed his sons in the small and struggling school maintained for the Lutheran minority.

His biographers have not always made it plain that he by choice identified himself not only with his ancestral Lutheran faith but also that he selected within the Lutheran fold a party—the party of the highly orthodox and the most conservative—for his own particular friends. Embarrassed, perhaps, that his hero, Bach, should deliberately have espoused the older orthodox party, Albert Schweitzer strove in his biography to remove from Bach the taint of rigid orthodoxy by

[15] David and Mendel, *op. cit.*, p. 125.
[16] Terry, *op. cit.*, p. 273. He owned both Latin and German editions of Luther's complete works.
[17] *Ibid.*, p. 116.

calling him "a mystic" who consorted with the rigidly orthodox not because of religious preference but from sheer necessity.[18] It seems, however, less damaging to Bach's reputation if we assume that he chose the rigidly orthodox within the Lutheran fold not merely from financial necessity but also because of personal conviction. At Mülhausen he found the church he served torn with dissension between the party of the Pietists (followers of Spener, and friends of the utmost simplicity in church music) and the party of the old orthodox, who approved elaborate figured music. Bach's own pastor at St. Blasius was addicted to the newer warmth in personal religion emanating from the Halle Pietists (the Spener-Francke group). But a newcomer on the local scene, a rival pastor, delivered several blasts against Pietism, and Bach sided in the controversy not with his own pastor but with minister of the other Mülhausen church (the Marienkirche). During the controversy Bach decided to leave Mülhausen; in his letter of resignation he defined his reasons: he had come to Mülhausen for only one purpose, the glorification of God by means of a well-regulated church music. The present disorders and vexations, he found, deterred him from the project which was nearest his heart; therefore he reluctantly felt obliged to go elsewhere; he wanted "the opportunity to pursue the object which concerns me most, the betterment of church music."[19]

Of course he never later found a perfect environment in any Lutheran church he served. But whatever his troubles, at least Arnstadt, Mülhausen, and later the

---

[18] Albert Schweitzer, *J. S. Bach* (London, 1923), I, 169.
[19] David and Mendel, *op. cit.*, p. 60.

churches at Leipzig provided him the essential oppor-
tunities he needed to compose and then perform.   A
casual reader may come across some such letter as the
one he wrote to his old friend, George Erdmann, Im-
perial Russian agent in Danzig during the 1730's, in
which he complained that the church authorities "are
odd and little interested in music, so that I must live
amid continual vexation, envy, and persecution. Should
Your Honour know or find a suitable post in your city
for an old and faithful servant, I beg you to put in
a most gracious word of recommendation for me."[20]
Someone may say—here is proof that Bach, even after
gaining the desired haven of a high-orthodox center in
Leipzig (where Pietism was discouraged and Calvinism
discountenanced), *still* chafed under his bit and wanted
to escape into freer reins.   But even at Danzig Bach
would have found only another Lutheran church, where
perhaps "continual vexation, envy, and persecution"
might not have dogged his steps.   Moreover, even during the years he was complaining most vociferously
about ill-treatment in Leipzig, the town council (which
controlled expenditures for music in the Leipzig
churches) was spending liberally.   The statement that
"so far as it was possible for the Council to paralyze the
creative faculty of his genius, it honestly tried to do
so,"[21] as Schweitzer already has shown, twists the facts.

Not by chance, then, but as the result of a happy conjunction in time of circumstances uniquely favorable was
Bach able to produce his masterpieces of church music.

[20] *Ibid.*, p. 125.
[21] Quoted in Schweitzer, *op. cit.*, I, 138.

Anterior to him was the favorable philosophy of church music enunciated by Luther and the priceless treasury of German chorales. Contemporary with him was a system of church finance in which whole blocks of churches were organized under one central spending agency, a council, whose duties included the engagement of a trained corps of musicians to perform in the several churches under its jurisdiction. In Leipzig, for instance, Bach realized (despite his constant plea of penury) about seven hundred thalers a year plus his living quarters, because he not only was director of music in one church but was responsible for the music in four churches. Leipzig in the middle of the eighteenth century was a town of 30,000. But in what town of 30,000 today would several churches, even of the same denomination, co-operate in paying the salaries of a group of professional musicians rotating among several churches?

Uniquely favorable to Bach also were the length and frequency of services in the Leipzig churches which he served. Taking as an example only St. Thomas Church, one discovers that during the early eighteenth century three services were held each Sunday and that the principal one lasted from seven in the morning until noon. The sermon (timed to last from eight until nine)[22] always developed a theme drawn from the Gospel appointed to be read for the day. The arrangement known as the "Leipzig Interim," moreover, provided for the use of vestments, lights, and the use of Latin for the principal portions of the liturgy. The Gloria, the Collect for the day, the Epistle, the Gospel, the Credo, the Pref-

[22] C. S. Terry, *Joh. Seb. Bach: Cantata Texts* (London, 1926), p. 25.

ace, and the Sanctus, for instance, were all said or sung in Latin. But Latin was no unknown tongue. Bach himself taught Latin for a time in the St. Thomas School; the third principal under whom Bach served, J. A. Ernesti, was an exceptionally brilliant student of the Latin classics.[23] Only within Bach's own lifetime did German gain a foothold in the University of Leipzig, where Thomasius was the first to lecture in the native language.[24] For those who did not understand Latin, prayer leaflets were provided in the Leipzig churches enabling the less well educated to follow the services in German.

Bach's choir assembled in the gallery of the church every Sunday morning about 6:45, during the playing of the organ prelude. After the organ music stopped, the choir then sang a short motet in Latin with words drawn from the Gospel appointed to be read for the day. The Latin motet chosen might be a composition by a Roman Catholic composer (such as Andrea or Giovanni Gabrieli, sixteenth-century organists at St. Mark's, Venice), or by a Lutheran composer (such as Bach's predecessor in the office of music director at St. Thomas, Calvisius). After the motet occurred an introit, and then the Kyrie; an external order of service was observed which did not differ conspicuously from the order of the Roman High Mass.[25] (Bach's masses with the

[23] See *Allgemeine Deutsche Biographie* (Leipzig, 1877), VI, 235-241. For further discussion of J. A. Ernesti's relations with Bach, see chap. vi, "Bach's Quarrel with the Rector of St. Thomas School."

[24] *Der Grosse Brockhaus* (Leipzig, 1934), XVIII, 638.

[25] Spitta, *op. cit.*, II, 264; III, 26.

exception of the *B Minor* were all clearly suitable for use in Lutheran Leipzig.)[26]

The most pronounced innovation in music during the early eighteenth century in conservative Leipzig churches was the sudden emphasis upon the cantata. The Bach cantata was essentially the musical counterpart of the sermon. The cantata text was drawn from contemporary religious verse in the majority of instances. At Leipzig it was frequently divided into two parts and inserted into the liturgy just before and after the hour-long sermon.

Again, then, we say: by a happy conjunction in time, Bach in the highly orthodox environment of early eighteenth-century Lutheranism possessed resources which Protestant composers have not often enjoyed. Handel did not write his oratorios for the church but for the concert stage, and during his entire lifetime never conducted any oratorio of his in a church. Mendelssohn, the composer of *Elijah*, also wrote for the concert stage, not for the church. Of the better-known "Protestant" religious masterpieces, only Bach's were written for presentation in church, as an integral part of Christian worship.

What shall be said, finally, about Bach's own personal religion? His predilection for theological reading is proved by the character of his library which at his death consisted exclusively of theological works.[27] He was consistently a student of Scripture; and his theological interests clearly transcended the polemical level. But

[26] *Ibid.*, III, 38.
[27] His theological library contained 83 volumes at his death; Tauler, A. H. Francke, Spener, and Johann Arndt were typical authors. See Spitta, *op. cit.*, III, 265-267.

the religious emotions which he dwelt upon with greatest earnestness were not always emotions that appeal to
modern liberal Christians. He loved, for instance, to
dwell on the blessedness of death, with the release it
brings. He developed themes drawn from the Song of
Solomon, allegorically treated, which do not always
appeal to moderns. He dwelt with harrowing zeal on
the horrors of hell and the everlasting awfulness of
damnation, themes not always emphasized nowadays.[28]
Since he had the choice of his own texts for the cantatas,
we may properly infer that those religious ideas which
recur incessantly in his cantatas (especially where no obvious relation to the Gospel for the Day can be seen)
represent the religious thoughts which he himself
especially endorsed.

"The art of the Bach cantata," we are told by one
author, "is an exposition of the foundations and principles of the Christian faith, and none more searching
or more inexorable, deeper or more precise has ever
been."[29] He plumbed the depths of religious emotion,
and his "artistic omnipotence," to use a phrase often applied to his music, sets him apart from all other composers who have treated sacred themes. His *Passion
according to St. Matthew* has been called the most sub-
lime music of history: enacting a "communal drama of
a compassion all-comprehending and an intuition un-
approachable." He is the "greatest of preachers since
Luther," and his music constitutes "one of the most
exalted temples ever constructed by the hand of man to

[28] See H. S. Drinker, *Index and Concordance to the Complete
Choral Works of Johann Sebastian Bach* (New York, 1942), pp.
18 (Death), 6 (Bride of Christ), 41 (Judgment Day).
[29] Einstein, *op. cit.*, p. 133.

the glory of God."[30]   In his greatest religious masterpieces he "miraculously realized all that was most complete, comprehensive, and objective . . . in the essence
and being of Christianity."

Because, however, Bach clung to the most conservative expression of the Christian faith, it is inevitable
that many churches today find his choral music, especially the cantatas, unacceptable, even when performance
resources are within reach.   Such a copious selection of
his short chorales as appears in the Harvard University
hymnbook, for instance, has been attained only because
it was found possible to fit to the music words express-
ing doctrinal standards other than those which inspired
Bach.   The task of finding other words for the larger
choral works, however, has proved more cumbrous.   His
instrumental music, lacking the embarrassment of
words, is oftenest played; the cantatas representing his
most intimate religious emotions, least often.   In the
concert hall his choral works are acceptable, since no
dogmatic meaning is extracted from the words.   The
concert artist can approach his music with no more concern for the dogma than a modern reader feels for the
celestial machinery in Homer's *Iliad*.   But in churches
the case is different, and a literal translation of the
words he set to music often proves unacceptable.

Another aspect of Bach's religious consciousness which
of necessity must separate his mentality from the typical
Protestant mentality today appears in his zealous devotion to liturgy.   With Bach "the observance of liturgy,
whether Catholic or Protestant, obviously mattered

[30] Karl Nef, *An Outline History of Music* (New York, 1935),
p. 227.

more . . . than the difference in denomination."[31]   Excessive reliance upon the Liturgical Year has never been a typical feature in American Protestantism.   His emphasis on musical symbols also separates him from us. His exposition of the Christian faith was not simply a matter of the texts he chose for his choral works: more emphatically it was an exposition in terms of certain musical symbols.   In his *Catechism Preludes* for instance, he endeavored to work out the formularies of Luther's entire *Shorter Catechism* by means of musical symbols, some of them only precariously understood.

But if his religious outlook seems remote, yet to the credit of the church he served is the fact that his masterpieces, now so vastly admired by secular musicians, were actually called into being at her behest.   Superintendent Deyling and Subdeacon Gaudlitz may have been odd and cantankerous, but at least the church they represented gave Bach the indispensable opportunity to produce.   Even if the old ladies did not like his music (and often they did not),[32] even if he felt underpaid, and even if his music did not always win friends and influence people among the Pietists who decried the sacramentarian system and disliked elaborate church music, at least his churches gave him his indispensable forum.

He expressed himself always for one end, *Soli Dei Gloria* ("for the glory of God alone").   Even his secular compositions bore that motto, along with the petition inscribed on nearly every piece he began, *Jesu juva*

[31] Manfred Bukofzer, *Music in the Baroque Era* (New York, 1947), p. 270.
[32] C. G. Gerber, *Historie der Kirchen-Ceremonien in Sachsen* (1732), p. 283 (translated in David and Mendel, *op. cit.*, p. 229).

("Jesus, help!").[33] At the end, as at the beginning, he
wanted above all else to walk into the presence of the
Eternal Light, and to find Him in whom there is no
variableness or shadow of turning. His last composition, a setting of an old chorale, expressed the yearning
of a lifetime:

> Before Thy throne, My God, I stand,
> Myself, my all, are in Thy hand;
> Turn to me Thine approving face,
> Nor from me now withhold Thy grace.
> Grant that my end may worthy be,
> And that I wake Thy face to see,
> Thyself forevermore to know!
> Amen, Amen, God grant it so![34]

[33] Terry, *Bach: A Biography*, p. 136.
[34] *Ibid.*, p. 264.

V. J. S. BACH'S "APPEALS TO CAESAR"

DURING BACH'S OFFICIAL CAREER AS a church musician he often appealed over the heads of his church superiors directly to secular authority, in order to win judgment in his disputes with his immediate church authorities. This annoying habit of his—appealing to Caesar—has in symbolical fashion persisted throughout the two centuries that have now elapsed since his death in July, 1750. Even today we find that Bach often appeals to the Caesars, that is to say, to the tsars of secular musical opinion, in order to force his way, an unwelcome guest, into the sanctuary. He does not present himself humbly and submissively with hat in hand, offering to act the willing handmaid in the sanctuary, but comes rather with a signed edict issued by the greatest musical critics, the elite of the secular music sphere, stating in categorical terms: *I am J. S. Bach, with special license to abide two whole centuries in my own hired dwelling, receiving all that come to me, preaching the kingdom of God with all boldness, but in my own way, none questioning my own particular methods.*

Before he went to Mülhausen, in fact during the very first years of his professional life, he set a pattern which he rather consistently maintained throughout his entire church career. In Arnstadt, where he held his first church appointment, he antagonized his fellow musicians; called one of them a "nanny-goat bassoonist," and according to the minutes of the consistory "had the

reputation of not getting along with the students."[1]
His musical innovations, even during those earliest years
at Arnstadt, caused consternation. The consistory reproved him "for having hitherto made curious *varia-
tiones* in the chorale, for mingling many strange tones
in it, and for the fact that the congregation has been
confused by it."[2] Threatening Bach with dismissal
from his post, the consistory (presided over by Superintendent Olearius of the Olearius family of Lutheran
divines) drew up a catalogue of complaints against the
young upstart:

The consistory desires to know where you have been for so
long, and who gave you leave of absence. . . . We are
surprised that you have given up performing figural music,
and conclude that the omission is due to your bad relations
with the pupils. . . . We must therefore ask you to tell us
explicitly that you are prepared to practice them in figural
music as well as in hymns. . . . You must tell us categor-
ically, yes or no, whether you will do what we require. If
you will not, we must find an organist who will.[3]

A few months were allowed by the lenient Arnstadt
Consistory to elapse after the first reproof of Bach, but
again in November, 1706, the consistory took action.
By this time Superintendent Olearius must have disapproved of Bach's very presence, for when the superintendent had called Bach's attention to the excessive
length of his organ pieces in church, Bach had turned
right around and "had at once fallen into the other

[1] Hans T. David and Arthur Mendel, *The Bach Reader* (New
York, 1945), p. 51.
[2] *Ibid.*, p. 52.
[3] C. S. Terry, *Bach: A Biography* (London, 1933), pp. 70-71.

extreme and had made it too short."[4]   As if to say: if
you will not accept my art on the terms I lay down,
you shall have nothing from me at all.

In any event, Bach was officially reproved again on
November 11, 1706, when the consistory set down in its
official minutes this comment: "If he considers it no disgrace to be connected with the Church and to accept his
salary, he must also not be ashamed to make music with
the students assigned to do so."[5]   Bach gave no answer
in apology, but said he would "declare himself in writing concerning this matter."   If his answer "in writing"
was ever forthcoming, there is no evidence for it in the
consistory archives, just as there is no evidence to show
that he replied in writing "within eight days" as he had
promised to do at the time of the first complaint made
against him several months previously.

And so Bach at his first church post in Arnstadt and at
his second church post in Mülhausen ended his official
connection with a resignation.   Well and good might it
have been for him to depart, symbolically wiping the
dust off his feet against Arnstadt and Mülhausen, and
at this distance it may seem the kingdom of heaven, if
superlative music is any criterion, had come very close
to those impercipient cities; doubtless, however, it will
be more tolerable for them than for Tyre and Sidon
in the judgment.   But Bach's sense of mission drove
him relentlessly on, always with the determination to
finish every task saying (as he did in his dedication of
the *Musical Offering*): "This resolve has now been
carried out as well as possible."[6]   Musical critics agree

[4] David and Mendel, *op. cit.*, p. 52 (excerpts from *Proceedings of
the Arnstadt Consistory*).
   [5] *Ibid.*, p. 53.   [6] *Ibid.*, p. 179.

that he completed every musical task "as well as possible," that is to say, as well as the task in hand could conceivably be accomplished. But the perfectionist zeal that consumed him made him an unwelcome guest in the household of the less zealous.

He shook off the dust of Arnstadt and Mülhausen, but in his last and greatest period, the quarter century that he spent at Leipzig, 1723-1750, Bach, though he may many times have chafed and looked elsewhere for a more soothing climate,[7] found no place else to move; he had done his last moving when he accepted appointment as Kuhnau's successor in the Leipzig post. Henceforth, having figuratively arrived at Jerusalem, he could do naught else but stay. Over and over again in Leipzig, however, he did what the Apostle Paul did when apprehended in the company of Trophimus. He tried throwing the chief priests into confusion by diverting issues, and then asserting that his disputes with his musicianly colleagues and church superiors arose only because "touching the hope and resurrection of the dead I am called in question." When he could not thus extricate himself, he followed an apostolic precedent and appealed to Caesar.

Caesar, in the case of eighteeth-century Leipzig, was at first Augustus II, King of Poland, Elector of Saxony, known as "the Strong." In order to secure the Polish crown he had abandoned his ancestral faith, and had embraced Catholicism; but though king of Poland, he normally resided in Dresden, some sixty-odd miles southeast of Leipzig. His one legitimate son followed him into the Roman Catholic Church, but the Lutheran

[7] Spitta, *Johann Sebastian Bach* (London, 1899), II, 253.

population of Saxony remained dominant in the realm. Augustus II, cordially disliked in Saxony because of his Polish affiliations, continued to reign for a decade after Bach's arrival in Leipzig. To him Bach addressed his first "memorial" in an effort to subvert the wills of local Leipzig authorities; after Augustus II's death in 1733, Bach then began appealing to Augustus III, another Roman Catholic Caesar, in order to reduce into submission his Leipzig Lutheran opposers. It would be unfair to Bach, of course, to omit mentioning that he always used his appeals to Caesar as a last resort, after all local efforts to protect his rights had failed.

The first appeal to Caesar occurred two years after his arrival in Leipzig. Bach had been in dispute with the governing authorities at the University of Leipzig from the moment of his installation as Cantor in Leipzig; the controversy centered in his right to conduct and oversee certain special services held at high festival times in the Paulinerkirche, the University Church. On the purely local level Bach succeeded in restraining a musical competitor of his, Görner by name, from directing at these traditional special occasions. But though the University Council was forced on the local level to restore Bach the directorship of these services at the Paulinerkirche, he was unsuccessful in his corollary demand for the salary of twelve florins traditionally paid for these annual services. Unable to get his fees, he dispatched the first in a series of complaints to Dresden, September 14, 1725. A reply from Dresden speedily arrived, stating that the University version differed substantially from his. Undaunted, he asked on November 3 for a copy of the University's allegations. Having received his copy, he then set to work drafting a third communication to his "potent and most gracious sovereign," the King-Elector, Augustus II. Dispatched December 31, this letter, one of Bach's lengthiest, displays not only a dogged determination to have his rights vindicated, but also a remarkable grasp of the legal technicalities involved in the dispute.[8] (Bach's son, Carl Philipp Emanuel, who took a law degree at the University, could have inherited a natural flair from his father.)

Bach won his contention, but his victory was a Pyrrhic one; his subsequent relations with the University authorities were embittered, and he never enjoyed the wholehearted co-operation from the University students which his predecessor in the Leipzig Cantorate, the more tactful Kuhnau, had received. Three carefully composed letters to Caesar had won him his first victory in Leipzig.

Following up his first success with a further cultivation of Caesar's favor, Bach conducted the next year an elaborate *Dramma per musica* extolling the virtues of the generally mistrusted Augustus II; a detailed account of this Leipzig event (May 12, 1727) tells of the presentation of a copy of Bach's *Dramma per musica* to His Royal Majesty "bound in deep scarlet velvet, with gilt tassels and gold fringes, but printed on white satin."[9]

Bach next collided with church authority over the choice of hymns for services at the Nicolaikirche, whose music (as well as that of the Thomaskirche) was under

[8] Terry, *op. cit.*, p. 183.
[9] David and Mendel, *op. cit.*, p. 110.

Bach's supervision. On September 8, 1728, the consistory of Leipzig issued an injunction requiring that Bach "when the ministers who are preaching cause it to be announced that particular hymns are to be sung before or after the sermon" be governed accordingly, "and have the same sung." Bach resented the choice of hymns made by a subdeacon who preached at the Nicolaikirche, complaining that the subdeacon chose "inordinately long" hymns, thus unduly extending the service and throwing it into confusion.[10] In this instance Bach must have been influenced by the fact that some of Paul Gerhardt's hymns chosen for singing reached thirty stanzas. Bach appealed from the consistory, which had taken the part of the subdeacon, to the civic town council, composed of laymen, not clergy.[11] The outcome is somewhat obscure, but Bach seems to have won his contention against the subdeacon.

Since the next few years found him in none too agreeable odor with his immediate superiors, he showed wisdom in seeking a cushion against their wrath to come. In 1733, Augustus II having died, Bach sent the Kyrie and Gloria of his *B Minor Mass* to the newly ascended sovereign, Augustus III, who from 1733 until Bach's death remained the ultimate secular authority. In dedicating the *B Minor Mass*, Bach came to the point soon enough after the necessary preliminary fanfare:

For some years and up to the present moment I have had the *Directorium* of the Music in the two principal churches in Leipzig, but have innocently had to suffer one injury or

[10] Terry, *op. cit.*, p. 194.
[11] The cantor's prerogative in choosing the hymns was "of long standing," as Bach pointed out to the Council.

another, and on occasion also a diminution in fees . . . but
these injuries would disappear altogether if Your Royal
Highness would grant me the favor of conferring upon me
a title. . . .

He did not specify the exact title he wanted, but he
asked for some honorary musical post in the Dresden
court, and furthermore requested that a certifying "document go forth to the proper place."[12]

Not until three years after the dedication of portions
of the *Mass in B Minor* to Augustus did Bach gain his
title. On December 1, 1736, the great organist Bach,
whose "feet flew faster than most performers' hands,
who never missed a note, who executed the most extravagantly difficult compositions with the ease and noncha-
lant perfection that ordinary performers can only bestow
on children's pieces," the "incomparable" Bach, "made
himself heard from 2 to 4 o'clock on the new organ in
the Frauenkirche, in the presence of the Russian ambassador."[13]

Since Augustus III, not "the Strong" like his father,
but weak, had been forced to haggle for the Polish
throne, and only after gaining Russian support had succeeded during June of 1736 in forcing his inglorious way
into Warsaw, he must naturally enough have been delighted when Bach, by every contemporary account one
of the most remarkable organists of all time, stunned
and excited the Russian ambassador, a connoisseur of
music. Bach had well earned his title, applied for three

[12] David and Mendel, *op. cit.*, p. 128.
[13] *Ibid.*, p. 151 (from the *Dresdner Nachrichten*). Count Kayserling, the Russian ambassador, later commissioned Bach to write
the famous *Goldberg Variations*, rewarding him for them with a
handsome goblet filled with gold coins.

years previously, when on December 1, 1736, he was selected to "stun and excite" the Russian ambassador. The title "His Majesty's Composer" was well earned: not only because he had sent portions of the incomparable *B Minor Mass*, not only because he had stunned the ambassador with his organ playing, but also because at what was apparently his own expense he had published librettos of several complimentary odes honoring the Dresden Royal Family during the three-year period of waiting for the title.

Earlier in 1736 a bitter feud, the full story of which will concern us in the next chapter, had broken out between Bach and J. A. Ernesti, head of St. Thomas School, where Bach trained his choristers. After more than a year of wrangling, with consistory and town council vainly striving to effect a reconciliation, Bach finally wrote a letter to Caesar—that is to say, Augustus III—appealing for aid, October 18, 1737. He had not acted suddenly in addressing Caesar this time, any more than he had acted precipitously in appealing to Caesar during the earlier dispute with the University authorities. The king's personal intervention in Bach's behalf at Easter time, 1738,[14] more than two years after the unfortunate contest had begun, finally stopped the flow of acrimonious letters.

A year before his death, the Leipzig town council was already canvassing a successor to Bach; at the meeting of the town council, only one week after his death, the councilors officially chose his successor. Burgomaster Stieglitz, Ernesti's staunch friend, arose at the council meeting, and without offering even a perfunctory trib-

[14] David and Mendel, *op. cit.*, p. 158.

ute to the memory of Bach, a small gesture of gratitude for his services, or a gracious expression to Bach's widow, offered instead the following oblique reference to Bach's services: "The School now needed a Cantor, not a Capellmeister."[15]   The man whom the council chose was a nonentity.   (Significant, too, was the interval of time which elapsed between Bach's decease and the new appointment—one week.   Bach, on the other hand, had had to wait ten months after the decease of his predecessor in the Leipzig post before securing election.)

Instinctively many churchmen turn from Bach now just because they do feel him to be a capellmeister (a concert musician) rather than a cantor (a church musician).   When finally Bach's masterpiece, the *St. Matthew Passion*, did receive a hearing one hundred years after its supposed entombment at Leipzig, it was revived, significantly, not in church, but in a concert hall.   Felix Mendelssohn, conductor at the revival, alluding for once to his Jewish ancestry, said on that occasion: "And to think it should be . . . a Jew who gives back to the people the greatest of Christian works."[16] Greatest of Christian works it may have been, may still be, but only in those churches today where the tsars of secular music opinion control the choice of church music does the *St. Matthew Passion*, or any other large Bach choral masterpiece usually gain a hearing.   Even today, then, he still appeals to the Caesars of secular music, and it is only their written approval that can hush the clamor of dissent that greets his music when untutored opinion is consulted.

[15] *Ibid.*, p. 189.   [16] *Ibid.*, p. 383.

And yet, his religious message cannot be fully savored except by those who share his basic outlook. His settings of the words of Jesus on the cross were intended to enhance the meaning of the words. The musician who simply regards the music, but not the text, can scarcely have received all that Bach meant to give. Whatever worldly success he may have achieved by his appeals to Caesar, his essential message is still germane only in a Christian society, and is still valid only in a Christian context. Perhaps our churches will one day therefore, even if not yet today, have the grace to receive him back into a more intimate fellowship, and his name shall be called Ishmael because the Lord has heard his afflictions, and he shall dwell with Abraham, and he shall not any more grow up in the wilderness.

VI. BACH'S QUARREL
WITH THE RECTOR OF
ST. THOMAS SCHOOL

ALTHOUGH BACH SPENT TWENTY-seven years in Leipzig as cantor, only the first decade of those twenty-seven years actually proved fruitful in the production of large-scale church works. During the first decade after his settlement in Leipzig Bach produced his *Magnificat*, his *Passion according to St. John*, his *Passion according to St. Matthew*, and composed also the music for the major portions of the *B Minor Mass*. His *Christmas Oratorio* was composed during 1734, but much of its music was derived from earlier secular cantatas.

During the last fifteen years of his life (from 1735 until 1750) Bach turned away from the writing of large-scale vocal works for church use. Handel, born the same year as Bach, wrote thirteen major oratorios on sacred subjects during that same period, 1735 to 1750. *The Messiah*, Handel's best-known oratorio, was first performed in 1742; Bach, however, during that same year completed not an oratorio but rather a set of thirty dazzling variations for double harpsichord, *The Goldberg Variations* (written to entertain an insomniac). And during the three-year period when Handel was writing *Judas Maccabaeus, Joshua, Solomon, Susanna,* and *Theodora*, Bach was occupying himself with the writing of ingenious variants on a musical theme composed by Frederick the Great of Prussia, and in the composition of recondite conundrums of a musical nature for *The Art of Fugue,* left unfinished at his death.

Were there external circumstances in the life of Bach which caused him to turn away from sacred composition of a choral nature? Albert Schweitzer, whose biography of Bach has exerted considerable influence, said: "In the case of no other artist has the external course of his life so little to do with the origin of his works, or is what we know of his life so insignificant, and, as regards his personal experiences, so uninteresting."[1] And because he believed external events had little influence on Bach's creativity Schweitzer paid them only slight attention. It will be our contention here, however, that Bach's quarrel with the rector of St. Thomas School (which flared up in 1736) did actually influence the whole tenor of his creative life, deflecting him from the composition of large-scale choral works to the writing of secular instrumental music.

Bach, who enjoyed amicable relations with the first two rectors under whom he served in the choir school from which he drew his singers, wrote large-scale vocal works while he was enjoying a measure of security in his relations with the student singers who performed the works. But when the third rector, J. A. Ernesti, through the powerful intercession of the mayor of Leipzig (in whose home he had lived) became head of the school in 1734, friction soon developed between rector and cantor; and after 1736 they were open enemies. "The situation between him and Ernesti developed to the point of charge and countercharge, and the two men

[1] Albert Schweitzer, *J. S. Bach* (London, 1923), I, 256.

from that time on [1736] were enemies."[2] The historian of St. Thomas School, J. F. Köhler, writing his history in 1776, forty years after Bach's falling-out with Ernesti, ascribed the continuously bad relations between rector and cantor during the forty-year intervening period (from 1736 until 1776) to the irreconcilable breach in 1736. After the breach Bach even "began to hate those students who devoted themselves completely to the *humaniora* and treated music as a secondary matter, and Ernesti became a foe of music."

Because Ernesti became a foe of music, Bach no longer had the kind of co-operation necessary for the practice and preparation of large-scale works. He then withdrew and devoted himself to the writing of the second volume of the *Well-Tempered Clavier*, *The Goldberg Variations*, and *The Musical Offering*, and other instrumental works. The only vocal works produced during the years after his breach with the rector and the consequent collapse of his own authority in the St. Thomas choir-school were his four "short" *Masses*, in part compiled from previously composed music.

The dispute between Bach and Ernesti arose over a question of authority in choosing musical assistants for the church services at St. Thomas Church and another church in Leipzig at which choristers from the Thomasschule regularly sang. The story is somewhat difficult to retell because two different students involved in the dispute bore the same surname, Krause. One of them had been placed in charge of singing at weddings. Unable to control the misbehavior of the boys chosen to

[2] Hans T. David and Arthur Mendel, *The Bach Reader* (New York, 1945), p. 137.

sing under his direction at weddings, he had caned some
of the worst offenders. Ernesti, hearing of his resort to
caning, announced that he should be publicly flogged before the whole student body. This particular Krause,
an exemplary youth of twenty-two, was at the moment
ready to enter Leipzig University, but choosing to
abandon all further hope of higher education rather
than submit to the public humiliation of a flogging he
fled the school, leaving behind certain possessions including thirty thalers; Ernesti, newly inducted as rector,
was himself twenty-nine at the time of the incident.
He was moreover a bachelor and evidently insecure
and high strung. He had been elevated to the prin-
cipalship of the school only two years previously and
owed his appointment, as everyone knew, to the personal intervention of Burgomaster Stieglitz,[3] under
whose aegis Ernesti sought always to shelter himself
when personally exercising authority. He was more
than twenty years younger than Bach, who was forty-
three when Ernesti first began to teach in St. Thomas
School. Ernesti when he began teaching was only
twenty-one; he was just a year older than Bach's own
eldest daughter. Sixteen years elapsed after he started
teaching before he finally married.[4]

To revert to the Krause incident, after flight Krause
attempted to recover his money and possessions but
Ernesti retained the money until an order from the
town council some weeks later forced him to restore the
money. In the place of the fugitive Krause another

[3] *Nova Acta Historico-Ecclesiastica* (Sechster Band, XLI-XLVIII
Theil) (Weimar, 1766), pp. 844-845.
[4] *Allgemeine Deutsche Biographie*, VI, 241.

student, also by the name of Krause, but unrelated (so far as is known), was temporarily elevated to the position of first prefect, that is to say, leader of the singing. After a time Bach discovered that the second Krause was incompetent and attempted to replace him. The second Krause meantime had obtained the favor of the rector, who decided he must on no account be dismissed from his new position of musical leadership. Bach, now fifty-one, told the twenty-nine year old rector that he preferred to choose his own musical assistants. Ernesti fell back on Burgomaster Stieglitz, nominal director of the school, and after openly flouting Bach announced to the students that anyone who acted even temporarily as leader of the choir in place of Krause (whom Bach sought to replace) would be summarily expelled from the school.

Bach took his case against Ernesti, whom he felt to be an interloper, first to the town council, over which Burgomaster Stieglitz presided, but received from them no satisfaction.[5] After a further period of tension during which time Bach lodged periodic complaints with the council in the vain hope of gaining a settlement, he took his case to the Leipzig consistory, but still without gaining satisfaction.[6] He then appealed to the King of Saxony, securing a resolution of the difficulty at the end of April, 1738, two years after it began. But although some kind of order verbally delivered from the king that the cantor was to be let alone seems to have been given in April, 1738, relations between Bach and Ernesti had in the intervening period so deteriorated

[5] David and Mendel, *op. cit.*, pp. 137 ff.
[6] *Ibid.*, pp. 153 ff.

that any later understanding or co-operation between the two proved impossible. After the breach Ernesti treated with discourtesy not only Bach but also those students who were particularly interested in music. His remark to a practicing student, "You want to become a beer-fiddler, too," has often been quoted as an instance of his disdain. Music was only one of Ernesti's aversions. He is also known not to have favored belles-lettres; he particularly disliked novels and plays of his own century, fearing that cultivation of new literature might lead to neglect of ancient writers.

His mission in life became that of a grammarian. His Latin texts (and he edited all the major Latin authors for school use) were among the most widely used school-texts of the eighteenth century. He worked with extreme rapidity, never polishing his editions of the classics; the copiousness of the notes, however, made them extremely popular, and he died a wealthy man from sales of his editions. He became a leader in the science of hermeneutics, and his text, *Institutio Interpretis*, 1761, was a landmark in New Testament criticism. Ernesti argued that in the interpretation of the Scriptures the same scientific principles should be used which are used to interpret any other writings of the ancient past. He was credited by Mosheim with founding the critical school which sought to "elicit the meaning of the Holy Scripture by the methods used in the interpretation and criticism of heathen writers," and Mosheim added that Ernesti's principles were "very soon carried to the length of denying any divine authority to the Bible."[7]

[7] J. von Mosheim, *Institutes of Ecclesiastical History* (London, 1863), III, 588.

As early as 1822, when Bach's name was still unknown in America, Ernesti was a light in theological circles, and a translation of his *Institutio Interpretis,* entitled *Elements of Interpretation,* was published by an Andover Seminary professor.[8] Although a nominal subscriber to the older formularies, Ernesti obviously preferred the outlook of the eighteenth century to that of the sixteenth. A typical student said of him that he "laid within me the immovable foundation of unbelief."[9] He wished to bring theology "to the touchstone of reason and philology," and his favorite target was the allegorical or anagogical interpreter of Scripture. "Ernesti scolded in a contemptuous manner, and mocked with bitter humour, over . . . visionary tendencies."

Goethe later studied under him, some years after Bach's death, during a period when Ernesti had risen to one of the most influential professorships in Leipzig University; but Goethe, though a hearer in one of his best courses on Cicero's *Orator,* went away unimpressed.[10] Jean Paul Richter, known in musical circles because of his influence on Robert Schumann, also studied under Ernesti, but passed this judgment on him: "With poor faculties of mind, he was astonishingly learned; but he owed his glory more to his industry than to his genius, more to his memory than to his depth. . . .

[8] Moses Stuart, *Ernesti's Elements of Interpretation* (Andover, Mass., 1822); this text was widely used in American seminaries, but was bitterly attacked in Alexander Carson's conservative *Examination of the Principles of Biblical Interpretation* (New York, 1855).
[9] Ch. Fred. Aug. Kahnis, *Internal History of German Protestantism* (Edinburgh, 1856), p. 134.
[10] *Allgemeine Deutsche Biographie,* VI, 237.

Most of the students were set in the direction of hetero-
doxy during Ernesti's time."[11]

Bach, unlike Ernesti, was a sincere devotee of the
old-fashioned kind of Lutheranism that stuck closely to
the Concordia Formula; it was this formula to which he
had subscribed before accepting the Leipzig cantorate.
That his subscription was far from perfunctory is demonstrated by the character of the library he had begun
gathering before he left Cöthen; allusion has already
been made to some of his most important holdings.
Of the twenty-seven authors represented, nearly all upheld a tightly orthodox Lutheran position. But Ernesti
would undoubtedly have anathematized such a book as
Adami's *Golden Apples* in which an interpretation of
the Song of Solomon was attempted along the allegorical lines popularized by Bernard of Clairvaux. Nine
books in Bach's library were written by August Pfeiffer,
the Oriental linguist who occupied a professorship at
Leipzig during the latter years of the seventeenth century; a linguist but not a piffling worrier over the discrepancies of Scripture (Ernesti worried over such matters as the discrepancies between John 19:14, Matthew
27:45, and Mark 15:25),[12] Pfeiffer was staunchly Lutheran in his respect for music as a discipline only a little
lower than that of theology itself.[13] Stenger's *Sermons*
in Bach's library extravagantly praised the organ and
the art of figural music.[14] (Ernesti, on the other hand,
opposed all church music of an elaborate type, because
he "found in it something that impaired scientific stud-

[11] Kahnis, *op. cit.*, p. 120.
[12] Stuart, *op. cit.*, pp. 89-90.
[13] Hans Preuss, *Bachs Bibliothek* (Leipzig, 1928), p. 125.
[14] *Ibid.*, p. 124.

ies."[15]) Heinrich Müller's *Love's Flame*, a devotional
work in his library, showed on the title page an organ
enclosed within a heart, fancifully showing the union of
the true devotional spirit with the love of organ music.[16]
All of Bach's other devotional books stressed the value
and necessity of observing the liturgical year.[17] A book
like Rambach's *Contemplations* suggested to him the
very order and arrangement of his choral cantatas.[18]
Everywhere in his choice he seized upon just those writings like Bünting's *Itinerary of Holy Scripture* that
would bring him closest to a devoutly reverential interpretation of Scripture. All the evidence at hand proves,
then, that Ernesti, whose first principle of interpretation
read: Treat the Scripture just as you would any other
piece of ancient literature,[19] stood at an opposite pole
from Bach's favorite authorities.

Ernesti's sermons in German were considered frigid,
and they probably reflected his personality. "As a person, he was stern and reticent." He was icily reserved
and "incapable of sympathizing with others' joys and
griefs."[20] His only show of pleasantness occurred in the
presence of Stieglitz or other rich persons whose sons
he delighted in instructing.[21]

In the throes of the controversy between the two
men, Bach wrote to the council: "If such irresponsible
conduct continues [Ernesti's usurpation of musical au-
thority] the services will be interfered with and the

[15] *Allgemeine Deutsche Biographie*, VI, 236.
[16] Preuss, *op. cit.*, p. 125.
[17] *Ibid.*, p. 122.
[18] *Ibid.*, p. 123.
[19] J. H. Kurtz, *Church History* (London, 1890), III, 146.
[20] *A. D. B.*, VI, 241.
[21] *Ibid.*, VI, 236.

church music fall into the most serious decay."[22]   He
added: "The School, too, within a short time [will]
suffer such deterioration as shall make it impossible for
many years to bring it back to its former estate."[23]
He founded his appeal also on the impairment of dignity in his office, which he foresaw might dangerously
impede the efforts of his successors.   He foresaw, as he
expressed himself to the Leipzig consistory, that without the co-operation of the student body (and the co-
operation of the rector) any further attempts at music
which required rehearsal would be impossible.   But
meantime Ernesti was not silent.   According to him,
Bach was a prevaricator and a liar, a venal cantor, moreover, who for a money bribe would declare a bass voice
to sing a sweet soprano.[24]   Because he was competent to
edit Cicero he fancied himself a suitable judge of the
technicalities of music, a subject which he had never
studied.[25]

However we may choose to regard Bach's own personal conduct during the affair, we are at least justified
in drawing from the controversy these several conclu-
sions: The personal controversy between the two men
flared after what may seem only trivial provocation; it
flamed hottest while Bach was still hoping to preserve
the traditional dignity of his office; after he reconciled
himself to the impossibility of changing Ernesti's attitude, he stopped writing in the larger choral forms
which had occupied him during his first years at Leipzig.

Ernesti—whose one daughter, rich and sought after,

[22] David and Mendel, *op. cit.*, p. 139.
[23] *Ibid.*, p. 139 (memorial dated Leipzig, Aug. 13, 1736).
[24] *Ibid.*, p. 147 (memorial dated Sept. 13, 1736).
[25] Philipp Spitta, *Johann Sebastian Bach* (London, 1899), III, 12.

was restrained from marriage, and instructed in Greek and Latin in order to provide him intellectual company—[26] himself died in 1781, at the age of seventy-three; still a spinster, she died soon afterwards. Robert Browning could have written Ernesti's epitaph:

> With the throttling hands of death at strife,
>> Ground he at grammar;
>> While he could stammer
> Still, through the rattle, parts of speech were rife. . . .

If we cannot endorse his attitude towards music, yet we can in oblique fashion thank him for sending Bach out from the church to write again for the world: such works as *The Goldberg Variations*, Parts II and III of *Clavierübung*, a sheaf of mighty Preludes and Fugues for Organ, and the *Musical Offering* are perhaps compensation for the loss of another *Matthew Passion*.

[26] *A. D. B.*, VI, 241.

VII. HANDELIAN ORATORIO

*T*HE *MESSIAH*, COMPOSED IN THE short space of twenty-four days during the late summer of 1741, was the work of a man in his fifty-seventh year. It was composed to an English text (drawn from Scripture), but Handel himself had never learned English so that he could speak it even passably well. Most of his career in England, where he had spent thirty years before writing *The Messiah*, had been taken up with the composition of a long list of Italian operas.

He began with *Rinaldo*, produced in London during 1711; nearly every year of the next two decades saw the London première of some new Italian work by Handel. During the scramble to hear Italian opera, John Gay wrote to Jonathan Swift (in 1723):

As to the reigning amusement of the town, it is entirely music. . . . There is nobody allowed to say, "I sing," but an eunuch, or an Italian woman. Everybody is grown now as great a judge of music, as they were in your time of poetry, and folks that could not distinguish one tune from another, now daily dispute about the different styles of Handel, Bononcini, and Attilio. . . . In London and Westminster, in all polite conversations, Senesino [a famous Italian eunuch] is daily voted to be the greatest man that ever lived.

During the years between 1728 and 1732, however, Handel's Italian operas were less successful. One after another *Siroe, Tolomeo, Lotario, Partenope,* proved a failure; they seemed to write inexorably on the wall the words: Mene, Tekel, Upharsin, the days of Italian opera are numbered, Handel is weighed in the balances and found wanting in public appeal, his kingdom is divided and given to Gay and Pepusch, writers of musical comedy. Handel could not change his lofty style; he could, however, change his medium. And while musical comedy pre-empted the affections of the volatile public, Handel tried a type of entertainment previously unknown in British music history—oratorio.

In 1732 he produced *Esther,* his first English oratorio, and made money from it. Reluctant, however, to admit irreparable failure, Handel again tried Italian opera—not once, but over and over again, hoping against hope for a success—between 1732, the year of *Esther,* and 1741, the year of the writing of *The Messiah.* The death knell of Italian opera had long ago sounded when Handel rang down the curtain on his last, and forty-second opera, *Deidamia,* in 1741. Handel, "a good old Pagan at heart,"[1] at last yielded to the inevitable, however, and spent the last ten years of his creative career (before blindness set in) entirely engrossed in the composition of oratorios.

Esther certainly did not originate from any profound spiritual hunger and thirst after the righteousness of sacred subjects. Much of the music in this first of Handel's English oratorios comes from an earlier masque written by him in 1720, *Haman and Mordecai.* In 1720 Handel had been in the employ of the Duke of Chandos, a war-profiteer, and it was for the Duke

[1] Edward FitzGerald, *Letters* (London, 1894), II, 49.

that the masque had originally been composed. In 1732
Handel seemed to have forgotten his 1720 masque,
but a friend who wished to honor him on his forty-
seventh birthday revived it in a private presentation;
the parts were acted by boys from the Chapel Royal
choir. The Earl of Egmont, who saw the private performance, wrote in his *Diary:*

From dinner I went to the Music Club, where the King's
Chapel boys acted the *History of Hester,* writ by Pope
[Alexander Pope] and composed by Handel; this oratorio
or religious opera is exceeding fine, and the company were
highly pleased, some of the parts being well performed.[2]

A little later in the same year a rival promoter, hoping to realize a profit from a public presentation of
Handel's masque, announced a public performance "at
the Great-Room in Villar's-street" for April 20. Handel
countered with an announcement of a performance, not
as originally composed for the Duke of Chandos, but
in a revised and enlarged form. The Children of the
Chapel Royal, who had sung—presumably in costume—
at the private presentation honoring Handel on his
forty-seventh birthday were not permitted to sing in the
public performance "by a great number of the best
Voices and Instruments" announced for May 2 at the
King's Theater; the Bishop of London, who was responsible for them, disapproved of a sacred opera given
in the commercial environment of the King's Theater.
    Esther, despite Bishop Gibson's disapproval, was suc-
cessful. Royal patronage, which had consistently be-

---

    [2] *Earl of Egmont MSS* (*Diary*) (Historical MSS Commission,
1920), I, 225.

friended Handel in England,[3] helped assure its success. The first public performance of *Esther* was announced with the prefatory phrase, "By His Majesty's command . . . will be performed the sacred story of Esther."

A contemporary critic stormed at Handel's "Religious Farce," masquerading as sacred oratorio, because: "the duce take me if I can make any other Construction of the Word, but he has made a very good *Farce* of it, and put near 4000*l* in his Pocket." Another wit satirized *Esther*, and expressed amazement that

> The Stage should yield the solemn Organ's note,
> And Scripture tremble in the Eunuch's throat.

But meantime Handel could sit calmly while his "Hallelujahs charmed the pious pit."[4] He could sit secure, knowing that however lethal might be the attack of bishops, he enjoyed the protection of royalty. Even after Handel died, the Hanoverian House remained staunch in support of his music; George III in particular conceived of himself as the "Protector of Handel." The great festival of 1784, and the final complete dominance which he achieved in British musical life was in no small measure attributable to George III's devotion to Handel, whose music though "laid aside as lumber after his death," was "taken up by a zealous and persevering party, and honoured in a singular way with royal patronage."[5]

[3] According to Newman Flower, *George Frideric Handel* (New York, 1948), pp. 119, 188, and 189, he enjoyed three different pensions of £200 each, the first bestowed by Queen Anne, the second by George I, and the third by George II.

[4] See R. M. Myers, *Handel's Messiah* (New York, 1948), pp. 25-27.

[5] Charles Burney, *A General History of Music* (London, 1789), IV, 414.

Handel's next essay in oratorio after *Esther* was
Athalia, founded on another Old Testament story. Produced first at Oxford in the summer of 1733, it proved
there and in London a resounding financial success. In
1736 he won the greatest plaudits of his middle period
with *Alexander's Feast*, whose libretto was by John
Dryden. According to the *London Daily Post* the first
night of *Alexander's Feast* brought in over £450; this
was his only large choral work printed in score during
his lifetime—testimony to its popularity. *Saul*, with
words by Charles Jennens, the same gentleman who was
later to compile the words for *The Messiah*, was composed during the summer of 1738; immediately after
finishing *Saul*, Handel turned to another large project,
Israel in Egypt.

In *Israel in Egypt* for the first time he restricted himself to the language of Scripture, and Scripture alone,
in choosing his text. It is not now known who compiled
the words for *Israel in Egypt;* Handel may have done
so himself. He had selected the Biblical texts for
George II's coronation music, brushing aside the offer
of any assistance in selection: "I have read my Bible
very well, and I shall choose for myself," he told the
Bishop of London. There were many felicities besides
the text in *Israel in Egypt*. The writing for double
chorus was especially impressive, and the delineation of
the plagues of Egypt has been admired for the pictur-
esqueness of the music.

The music owed much to prior Italian models, and
certain portions were merely refurbished rather than
freshly composed by Handel. Plagiarism was by no
means uncommon in eighteenth-century musical life;

one of Handel's rivals in opera, an Italian named Bononcini, rifled a madrigal by another Italian, Lotti, but was detected in his purloining of Lotti's music. Discredited in London on account of the discovery of his theft, Bononcini was driven away in ignominy. Handel, however, when he lifted music from Stradella, Erba, Urio, or any other Italian, generally improved the music he borrowed, and therefore perhaps deserves praise rather than censure for rescuing from oblivion the inspirations of lesser men.

In *The Messiah* itself Handel did not scruple in his borrowing; but he showed considerable discrimination—he borrowed only from himself, using certain earlier compositions with Italian text. The music for the famous chorus "For unto Us a Child Is Born," was originally music which he composed for the words (in Italian): "No, I will not trust you, blind Love, cruel Beauty! You are too treacherous, too charming a deity!" The Scriptural words "Unto us a Son is Given" are set to music which Handel originally wrote for the line "Blind Love, cruel Beauty!" The music which he set to the text "And He Shall Purify the Sons of Levi" was originally conceived by him for Italian words meaning "Life too is a flower; it comes up with the morn and dies with the spring of a single day." The chorus "His Yoke Is Easy" uses music originally set to an Italian text: "The flower that laughs in the rosy dawn withers in the sunlight and sinks into the grave at evening." Another instance of the tribute that Handel levied on his secular Italian duets occurs in the chorus "All We Like Sheep Have Gone Astray."[6] In all these

[6] Sedley Taylor, *The Indebtedness of Handel* (Cambridge, 1906), pp. 36-46.

borrowings from himself (and in other instances of borrowing from others) he happily bestowed significance upon music that in its earlier guise commanded less respect.

Handel first produced his *Messiah* in Dublin; as with all his other oratorios the environment of the first performance was not a church but a theater. Some assistance with the choral portions was provided by singers drawn from St. Patrick's Cathedral Choir, by gracious permission of the Dean of St. Patrick's, Jonathan Swift. Tickets for the first performance, proceeds of which went to charity, sold for half a guinea each. Approximately eight hundred persons heard the first performance, which received hearty applause from "a most Grand, Polite, and Crowded Audience."

As with all of Handel's oratorios, *The Messiah* was called an "Entertainment" in the press notices. Charles Jennens, who compiled the words provides further authority for calling it an entertainment. Speaking of the texts, he said: "I shall show you a collection I gave Handel, call'd *Messiah,* which I value highly, and he has made a fine Entertainment of it, tho' not near so good as he might or ought to have done." In London, as in Dublin, *The Messiah* was accounted entertainment, not edification.

Several days after the first exhibition of the same divine oratorio, Mr. Handel came to pay his respects to Lord Kinnoul with whom he was partially acquainted. His lordship, as was natural, paid him some compliments on the noble entertainment which he had lately given the town.[7]

[7] Sir William Forbes, *Life and Writings of James Beattie, LL.D.* (London, 1824), II, 62.

For Mrs. Cibber, the contralto soloist at the first Dublin performance (and later soloist in the London performances), Handel is said expressly to have written the now-famous aria, "He Was Despised and Rejected of Men." She had left her husband, Theophilus Cibber, in order to live with a paramour, and on other accounts her reputation was less than immaculate. At the first Dublin performance, where news of her vagaries had preceded her, one clergyman, enthralled by her singing of "He Was Despised," arose and said in a loud voice: "Woman, for this be all thy sins forgiven thee!" The other singers whom Handel used in his London season beginning February 18, 1743 (during which he brought out both *Samson* and *The Messiah*, giving the latter, however, under another title) were singers who, like Mrs. Cibber, were trained for the playhouse and not the church.

The incongruity of making a public entertainment out of the life of Christ, and seeking therefrom a profit, offended many. The clergy were outspoken in protest, and Handel, in order to mollify them, disguised *The Messiah* at its first London performance under a new title, *A Sacred Oratorio*. For six years after its first presentation *The Messiah* was heard in London only as *A Sacred Oratorio*. In time clerical protest died, and a year before Handel's death a liberal clergyman like John Wesley listened to it and praised it.[8] George II, loyally doing what he could to overcome opposition, attended the first London performance, and set a precedent by standing during the "Hallelujah Chorus." Only after Handel began his association with the

[9] John Wesley, *Journal*, Curnock ed. (London, 1938), IV, 282.

Foundling Hospital (to which he utlimately bequeathed the performing rights of *The Messiah*) did *The Messiah* achieve any notable popularity with London audiences. In 1749, six years after its first London performance, he was able to advertise it under its rightful name. And in 1767, eight years after his death, the score was finally printed.

The Messiah uses for its libretto a total of eighty verses from Scripture. Only ten of these eighty verses are from the Gospels, though the title of the oratorio indicates Christ as the central figure. The largest number of verses in the libretto from any one single book in the Bible are taken from Isaiah; the second largest number from Psalms. Thirty-seven verses, almost half the total, are selected from these two books. Haggai, Zechariah, Malachi contribute seven verses to the libretto; these three minor prophets in conjunction with Lamentations and Job contribute a number of verses—ten—which equals the total number of verses chosen from the Gospels.

For this libretto Handel was indebted to Charles Jennens, whom Dr. Johnson called "a vain fool crazed by his wealth." Dr. Johnson added that if Jennens were in Heaven, he "would criticize the Lord Almighty." He lives, Johnson said, "surrounded by all the luxuries of an Eastern potentate, verily an English 'Solyman the Magnificent'; who never walks abroad without a train of footmen at his heels, and, like Wolsey, with a scented sponge 'neath his nose, lest the breath of the vulgar herd should contaminate his sacred person."[9] But Jennens, despite his boundless self-esteem, won Handel's complete respect.

Handel set three of Jennens's librettos, the third, *Belshazzar*, representing in its own fashion as great an achievement as the libretto of *The Messiah*. In *Belshazzar* Jennens combined the fifth chapter of Daniel with the historical hints concerning the fall of Babylon contained in Xenophon's *Cyropaedia*. Cuneiform inscriptions confirm that Belshazzar was, if not a king, recognized as the son of a king; archeological research has demonstrated, moreover, that the conquest of Babylon was accomplished as Xenophon stated, by Cyrus, not Darius (Daniel infers that Darius overcame Belshazzar). Founding his interpretation on Isaiah 45 as well as Daniel 5 Jennens (who presupposes a lacuna of several years between Daniel 5:30 and 31) prepared a libretto whose poetry limps, but whose scholarly foundations are sturdy. As a character study it has distinct merit: Gobryas, a character from Xenophon, is assigned a valid reason for his treachery to Belshazzar.

Handel's oratorios other than *The Messiah* and *Israel in Egypt* use poetical librettos. *Samson*, written immediately after *The Messiah*, uses a libretto modeled on *Samson Agonistes*; bits from Milton's *On the Nativity*, *On the Passion*, *On Time*, *At a Solemn Music*, *Epitaph on the Marchioness of Windsor*, and added material from his psalm-paraphrases, thrown together, constitute the libretto. Despite the superior quality of some of

[9] Flower, *op. cit.* p. 271 n. This quotation from Dr. Johnson, though extremely colorful, may be apocryphal. Flower does not give his source.

the poetry remodeled for *Samson,* such passages as the
following are now objectionable:

> To man God's universal law
>   Gave pow'r to keep his wife in awe.
> Thus shall his life be ne'er dismay'd,
>   By female usurpation sway'd.

The chorus, "Fix'd in His Everlasting Seat," impar-
tially praises Jehovah and Great Dagon with the same
strains of music, sung antiphonally. Modern conscience
would prefer a different kind of musical praise addressed to Dagon and Jehovah. Samson's air "Why
Does the God of Israel Sleep?" is questionable because
in it he implores God to arise with a dreadful sound, to
raise a tempest of wrath, to pursue with whirlwinds full
fraught with vengeance the heathen, till shame and
trouble seize them. The tone is that of the imprecatory
psalms.

Samson was in Handel's opinion a better oratorio
than the *Messiah;* unfortunately the virtues of the Old
Testament are not today relished as they once were.
In his epoch many Britishers identified themselves with
the true Israel, and therefore were able to apply the
Old Testament invective to their own foes. The miracles of the Old Testament also find today less literal
acceptance. Handel's *Joshua* pictures three miracles in
succession—the passing over Jordan dryshod, the fall of
the walls of Jericho after a sevenfold encompassing and
the blowing of trumpets, and finally the standing still
of the sun. Interspersed with these the libretto devel-
ops a love affair between Othniel and Achsa. In
Jephtha a trumped-up love affair between Jephthah's

daughter, Iphis, and a fictitious warrior, Hamor, is developed at considerable length. At the end of *Jephtha* "an Angel appears, and forbidding the sacrificial rites to proceed, declares that Iphis shall be devoted to a life of celibacy and service to God." The oratorio *Joseph and His Brethren* also works out in a somewhat fanciful way Joseph's amorous exchanges with "Asenath, daughter to Potiphera, High Priest of On." But this particular love affair would necessarily lack intensity in a modern presentation because, according to Handel's direction, Joseph's part must be sung by a male contralto. The part of Solomon in the oratorio of the same name (although Solomon vigorously prosecutes his love affair with Pharaoh's daughter, according to the oratorio plot) must also have been sung by a eunuch, a male alto. Joacim, Susanna's husband in *Susanna*, is a male alto part. Cyrus and Daniel in *Belshazzar* are both male contralto parts.

The reasons that now militate against the presentation of Handel's other oratorios, even though he himself may have felt the music of some of the others to be better than the music of *The Messiah*, begin to show themselves. And he was not alone in thinking *The Messiah* music less interesting; in 1758 a learned critic declared that *Samson* must always stand first among Handel's works.[10] Sir John Hawkins, one of the most perspicacious admirers of Handel, declared that the airs in *The Messiah* "were greatly inferior to most in his operas and former oratorios." Charles Burney, the other famous music historian of the eighteenth century, said: "The Overture to the *Messiah*, though grave and

[10] Myers, *op. cit.*, p. 147.

solemn, always seemed to me more dry and uninteresting . . . than the rest of Handel's Overtures."[11]   But even if informed musicians have preferred *Jephtha*, for instance, or *Samson*, or any of the others, public performance of these others is usually out of the question today.

An oratorio like *Saul*, despite musical beauties, clearly cannot be presented today if its libretto is taken seriously.   Merab, Saul's daughter, after hearing Jonathan praise David, sings: "What abject thoughts a prince can have!   In rank a prince, in mind a slave!   Yet think," she tells Jonathan, "on whom this honor you bestow, how poor in fortune, in birth how low!"   In gratitude for David's saving Israel from the Philistines, Saul proposes a marriage between David and Merab, but she scornfully rejects the shepherd upstart with these lines: My soul rejects the thought with scorn, that such a boy, till now unknown, of poor, plebeian parents born, should mix with royal blood his own!   Though Saul's commands I can't decline, I must prevent his low design, and save the honor of his line.

Judas Maccabaeus and *Alexander Balus* are both unwelcome today because their stories, taken from apocryphal I and II Maccabees are not esteemed.   Handel wrote these oratorios in order to curry Jewish favor, and he was at the time highly successful with *Judas Maccabaeus*, at least.   But *Alexander Balus* is again embellished with a fanciful love story involving the hero and Cleopatra.   Demetrius, Ptolemeus, Alexander, and Cleopatra, all figure in I Maccabees 10-11, but who in a

---

[11] Charles Burney, *An Account of the Musical Performances in Westminster Abbey* (London, 1785), p. 74.

Protestant church today reads Maccabees? Large
stretches of the Old Testament are *terra incog-
nita;* and the bald emphasis on miracles without ethical
meaning and the interpolation of contrived love affairs
offend contemporary taste.

Beethoven said that Handel was the greatest composer that ever lived, adding, "I would uncover my
head, and kneel before his tomb."[12] "There is truth,"
he said when presented with a forty-volume edition of
Handel's works. When Haydn heard a selection from
Joshua, he said that he "was perfectly certain that only
one inspired author ever did, or ever could, pen so sub-
lime a composition." Glück said, "I look upon him with
reverential awe."

Yet, despite the acknowledged pre-eminence of
Handel, he is today a neglected composer. *The Messiah,* though frequently performed, cannot adequately
expose his genius to the inquiring public. A step in the
right direction will perhaps have been made when he is
frankly recognized as no church composer; his *Messiah*
after all remains in the church repertory not because
the music is inherently so much more enduring in value
than the music of the other oratorios, but simply because
the words are not offensive to modern "enlightened"
conscience. His only other Christian oratorio, *Theodora,* cannot win general acceptance in church circles;
its hagiological aroma tells against it.

But Handel may yet triumph despite his outmoded
eighteenth-century texts. His operas, long forgotten,
have been successfully revived during the past quarter

[12] Percy M. Young, *Handel* (London, 1947), p. 177.

century. In a concert hall, where they belong, his now unperformed oratorios may also prove to be musical, even if not devotional, masterpieces; certainly if we are to know him as we know Beethoven or Bach the time must soon come when his other oratorios begin again to be heard.

VIII. DR. WATTS'S "FLIGHTS OF FANCY"

W ATTS HAS OFTEN BEEN CALLED the "father" of the English hymn. As with so many generalizations, this concept of Watts as the first hymn writer provides an oversimplification of his essential achievement. During his own lifetime Watts "could have compiled an English hymnbook out of existing materials, whose excellence would not be questioned today."[1] The distinctive achievement of Dr. Watts was not his fathering of the English hymn; hymns by Herbert, Herrick, Donne, Ken, Baxter, many of them suitable for congregational singing, had been written long before Watts issued his first volume of *Hymns* in 1707. Why then has he been called the "Father of the English Hymn"?

Not everyone who nowadays sings his hymns realizes that Watts appeared at a time when hymn singing as such was still strenuously opposed in Established and Dissenting Churches both in England and in Scotland. The prejudice against hymn singing as a part of congregational worship drew impetus from a reading or misreading of New Testament injunctions on the conduct of public worship. In Watts's day, sanctified by an unbroken custom handed down from the middle of the sixteenth century, the singing of the Psalms of David and certain other Scriptural canticles furnished the only congregational exercise allowed in the vast majority of

[1] Percy Dearmer, *Songs of Praise Discussed* (London, 1933), p. xvii.

churches. Watts's peculiar mission was the undermining
of this long-established custom, and, paradoxically
enough, the petard he used was his own *Psalms of
David Imitated in the Language of the New Testament*.
Watts's "Imitations" were imitations in the eighteenth-
century sense, and David provided him only with a
convenient and acceptable point of departure. He pro-
ceeded on the theory that "by keeping too close to
David in the House of God, the Vail of Moses is thrown
over our Hearts."[2] Sensing the restiveness of English
congregations who chafed under the "Vail of Moses,"
he set about "correcting and refining" the royal bard's
poetry.

His excuse for correcting and refining David's rhap-
sodic effusions was contained in the preface to his 1719
volume. David's poetry, Watts tells us, frequently be-
trays a certain "cloudy Jewishness" which must be rem-
edied by the injection of the "clearer revelations" of
the Gospel. Watts excises David's cloudy Jewishness in
Psalm II and gives his improved version the title,
"Christ's Dying, Interceding, and Reigning." Psalm
VIII becomes a poem entitled "Adam and Christ, Lords
of the Old and New Creation." Psalm XIII is entitled
"The Promise and Sign of Christ's Coming." "Christ's
All-Sufficiency" is the title of Psalm XVI, and similar
improvements are made throughout the remainder of
the volume. Because of the liberties he took with the
original text, his imitations aroused conservative protest.
But many churches nevertheless re-echoed a long amen

[2] I. Watts, *Hymns and Spiritual Songs . . . With an Essay Towards the Improvement of Christian Psalmody* . . . (London, 1707),
p. v.

after Watts's tirade against the royal psalmist and took up his imitations with alacrity. By the end of the eighteenth century, as one critic put the case, "Christian congregations [had] shut out divinely inspired Psalms," and in their place had "taken in Dr. Watts's flights of fancy,"[3] always proceeding, of course, on the theory that the singing of David's Psalms constituted a divinely revealed ordinance. In the period of the Great Awakening this procedure enabled the churches to have their cake and eat it too. They were able to solace themselves with the comforting thought that they were adhering to the faith once delivered to the saints, and yet rejoice in having a large body of poems at hand which stressed the cardinal truths of the gospel. Watts, who was no paltry scholar, knew always just what he was doing: "If some readers should suppose the English verse here to mistake the Hebrew sense, yet perhaps these evangelical allusions . . . may be more agreeable and useful to the Christian worshipper."[4]

Watts, who repeatedly expressed his admiration for John Dryden, patterned his psalm-imitations on earlier models of imitation found in the works of Cowley (the Pindaric imitations) and of Dryden. Dryden's definition of imitation is relevant:

I take imitation [*Preface to the Translation of Ovid's Epistles*] . . . to be an endeavor of a later poet to write like one who has written before him, on the same subject; that is, not to translate his words, or to be confined to his sense,

[3] William Romaine, *The Whole Works* (London, 1787), p. 990.
[4] I. Watts, *The Works of the late Reverend and Learned Isaac Watts . . . Now first published from his Manuscripts . . . revised and corrected by D. Jennings . . . and . . . P. Doddridge . . .* (London, 1753), IV, 79.

but only to set him a pattern, and to write as he supposes the author would have done, had he lived in our age, and in our country.[5]

In the case of David's Psalms, Watts cavalierly omitted as "unworthy of paraphrase" a dozen psalms, and in order to make "David speak like an eighteenth century British Christian,"[6] so altered a score of others as to render them unrecognizable.

Watts highly disapproved of the vengeful, vindictive note struck in many of the Psalms of David. In random footnotes throughout the "Imitations" one finds such comments as these: "I have here omitted the dreadful imprecations on his enemies";[7] "Rejoicing in the destruction of our personal enemies is not so evangelical a practice, therefore I have given this verse [of the psalm] another turn";[8] "The particular complaints of David against Achitophel here are entirely omitted. . . . I have also left out some whole psalms . . . that tend to fill the mind with overwhelming sorrows or sharp resentment";[9]—and Watts therefore in his own delightful way went about brightening "by the clearer discoveries of the gospel" the "composures of the Jewish psalmist."

In his endeavor to bring David up to date, Watts furthermore changed the psalms in order to harmonize

[5] Flora R. Amos, *Early Theories of Translation* (New York, 1920), p. 151.

[6] John Dryden in his preface to the *Aeneid* had announced a similar purpose: "I have endeavored to make Virgil speak such English as he would himself have spoken, if he had been born in England, and in this present age" (*The Works of John Dryden*, Scott-Saintsbury ed., Edinburgh, 1889, XIV, 220).

[7] Watts, *The Works* (1753), IV, 66.

[8] *Ibid.*, IV, 86.

[9] *Ibid.*, IV, 54.

them with prevailing economic attitudes of the eighteenth century. Where the psalmist had scored usury, Watts

thought it necessary also to leave out the mention of usury, which though politically forbidden by the Jews among themselves was never unlawful to the Gentiles, nor to any Christians since the Jewish polity expired.[10]

Watts, who throughout his long life always preferred to live at the sumptuous country estate of a former London alderman (his health demanding the country air), tactfully omitted the mention of those "temporal" blessings which the royal psalmist repeatedly promised the righteous, because as he expressed it, he believed in

discouraging a too confident expectation of these temporal things, . . . the positive blessings of long life, health, recovery, and security in the midst of dangers . . . so much promised in the Old Testament, and so little in the New.[11]

He considered it better for the "vulgar Christians, the meanest of 'em," as he patronizingly referred to them in the preface to the 1719 volume, to concentrate on the promise of "heavenly hopes, more agreeable to the Gospel."[12]

The happy land of Canaan in Watts's "Imitations" becomes the British Isles. After omitting the Davidic promises of such personal blessings as long life, health, recovery, and security amidst dangers, because these promises do not appear in the New Testament, he then magnified stray hints of Canaan's blessings into huge

[10] I. Watts, *The Psalms of David Imitated in the Language of the New Testament* (London, 1719), p. 39.
[11] Watts, *The Works* (1753), IV, 40.
[12] *Ibid.*

prophecies of Britain's future greatness. His version of
Psalm LXVII contained, for instance, the following
lines:

Shine, mighty God, on Britain shine . . . God the Redeemer
scatters round His choicest favors here . . . Sing loud with
solemn voice,/ While British tongues exalt his praise,/ And
British hearts rejoice![13]

He changed Psalm LXXV into a series of Anti-Jacobite
invectives.[14]   The title read: "Power and government
from God alone, Applied to the Glorious Revolution by
King William, or the happy accession of King
George to the throne."   In another place he called King
George II a "royal saint," and saluted him with the
couplet:

> 'Tis George the Blest remounts the throne,
> With double vigor in his son.[15]

Watts, in a version of Psalm C, wrote this stanza:

> Sing to the Lord with joyful voice
> Let every land his name adore;
> The British Isles shall send the noise
> Across the ocean to the shore. . . .[16]

And in Psalm CIV he developed a similar theme: "O
bless his name, ye Britons!"[17]   Psalm CXV exhorted:
"O Britain, trust the Lord."[18]   And Psalm CXLVII
elaborated reasons for praising and trusting the Lord:
"O Britain, praise thy mighty God. . . .   He bid the

[13] Watts, *The Psalms* (1719), p. 170.
[14] *Ibid.*, pp. 195-196.
[15] I. Watts, D. D., *Reliquiae Juveniles; Miscellaneous Thoughts in Prose and Verse* . . . (Glasgow, 1786), p. 219.
[16] Watts, *The Psalms* (1719), p. 256.
[17] *Ibid.*, p. 271.   [18] *Ibid.*, p. 303.

ocean round thee flow; No bars of brass could guard
thee so."[19]   A little later in this last poem Watts con-
trasted British customs with foreign ones to the ad-
vantage, of course, of Britain: "He [God] hath nobler
ways,/ To call the Britons to his praise."

Not content with justifying the ways of God to the
British in England alone, Watts found a new title for
the last part of Psalm CVII: "Colonies planted; or
Nations blest and punish'd; A Psalm for New England."[20]   Two stanzas give an idea of the author's manner in this compliment to the New World:

> Where nothing dwelt but beasts of prey,
> Or men as fierce and wild as they,
> He bids th'oprest and poor repair,
> And builds them towns and cities there.
>
> Thus they are blest; but if they sin,
> He lets the heathen nations in,
> A savage crew invades their lands,
> Their princes die by barb'rous hands.

Doubtless there were New Englanders as there were
Britishers who thanked him for his "brightening" of the
psalms with the clearer revelations of the Gospel, but
there were, however, at least a few abroad who continued to prefer David to Watts.   "Compared to the Scripture," wrote one conscientious divine, "they are like a
little taper to the Sun; as for his Psalms, they are so
far from the mind of the Spirit, that I am sure if David
were to read them, he would not know any one of them
to be his."[21]   And the same author continues: "Why

[19] *Ibid.*, pp. 386-387.   [20] *Ibid.*, p. 286.
[21] W. Romaine, *op. cit.*, p. 999.

should Dr. Watts . . . not only take precedence of the
Holy Ghost, but thrust him entirely out of the Church?
Insomuch that the rhymes of a man are now magnified
above the word of God."[22]

By the time these criticisms reached the public (the
year before the American Revolution) Watts had won
the vast majority of English and American churches to
his side, and his Trojan Horse technique had opened
wide the closely guarded gates of the Christian system
of praise; where previously the singing of divinely appointed Psalms of David had formed the sole vehicle
of congregational praise, first his poems masquerading
as Psalms of David were wheeled within the Christian
walls, and then there had emerged a full flood tide of
"hymns of human composure." His volume of psalm
imitations (placed before the public in 1719) contained
such "psalms" as that great missionary favorite of congregations today: "Jesus Shall Reign Where'er the
Sun," certainly an advantageous hymn, but hardly
Psalm LXXII; and "Joy to the World," the well-
known Christmas favorite, but hardly a version of
Psalm XCVIII, when the words contain even less of
David than the tune does of Handel.

His excuse was that he was "forced" to issue these
hymns as psalms. He wrote confidentially to a friend,
Dr. Colman of Boston, some twenty years after the
publication of his "Imitations": "I must say that I
imitated David's Psalms, not as the fittest book that
could be made for Christian worship, but as the best
which the churches would yet hearken to."[23] Writing

[22] *Ibid.*, p. 990.
[23] *Massachusetts Historical Society, Proceedings,* 2nd series
(Boston, 1895), IX, 365.

to the same friend again, Watts further emphasized his general stand:

I see the sense of the people of New England, how necessary it is to keep near the original, i. e. in my opinion how necessary it is to sing something Jewish and something personal belonging to David. . . . But I repeat these words out of my preface to the large edition of my Imitation of the Psalms, "Still I am bold to maintain the great principle on which my present work is founded, and that is, that if the brightest genius on earth or an angel from heaven should translate David, and keep close to the sense and style of the inspired author, we would only attain thereby a bright or heavenly copy of the devotion of the *Jewish* [Watts's italics] King, but it would never make the fittest song-book for a Christian people."[24]

With Alexander Pope in his famous translation of Homer, it would appear that Watts shared the honor of having made some "very pretty poems," but with less justification than Pope in attaching the name of another author to his pretty poems: because unlike Pope he set about his task consumed with little inner loyalty to the Davidic material, but only because he found the churches would "hearken to nothing" without the Davidic title. In this case it was not a case of the rose smelling as sweet by another name, but rather another flower by the name of rose smelling sweeter. Watts achieved his end; what Dr. Johnson said on another occasion of Pope might just as well have been referred to Dr. Watts: "To a thousand cavils one answer is necessary; the purpose of a writer is to be read, and the criticism which would destroy the power of pleasing must be blown aside."[25]

[24] *Ibid.*   [25] F. R. Amos, *op. cit.*, p. 165.

We may cavil along with Dante Gabriel Rossetti, who a century ago expressed his ideas on "pleasing" when he wrote:

The work of a translator is one of some self-denial. . . . Sometimes a flaw in the work galls him, and he would fain remove it, doing for the poet that which his age denied him; but no—it is not in the bond.[26]

To us nowadays "there seems a real question of intellectual honesty involved," and we feel that we must "beware lest a translation of a man's work be not really a questionable procuring, not to say a forging, of his signature to some modern manifesto,"[27] but all such cavils, if we are to follow Dr. Johnson, must be blown aside if fidelity to the meaning of the author "destroys the power of pleasing."

A popular balladeer of the early eighteenth century expressed the idea:

Hang Homer and Virgil; their meaning to seek,
A man must have poked into Latin and Greek;
Those who love their own tongue,
        we have reason to hope,
Have read them translated by Dryden and Pope.[28]

There were also spirits abroad in the land who were ready to "Hang David," and who thanked Watts in the following general terms:

For when the rich original we peruse
And by it try the metal you produce,

[26] Quotation in Amos: D. G. Rossetti, Preface to *Translations* (n.d.), p. xiv.
[27] J. S. Phillimore, *Some Remarks on Translation and Translators* (Oxford, 1919), p. 16.
[28] Amos, *op. cit.*, p. 173.

> Though there indeed the purest ore we find,
> Yet still by you it something is refined.[29]

Watts himself would no doubt have agreed that he refined the ore, though it seems possible he would have
resented the phrase, "*purest* ore."[30]

As important as were the psalm-imitations, yet any
just estimate of Watts's achievement in verse must at
least comprehend two other principal volumes, *Horae
Lyricae* (1706), and *Hymns and Spiritual Songs*
(1707); perhaps also a third which eventually attained
an astounding vogue, *Divine and Moral Songs* (1715),
containing hymns for children, should be studied.
Horae Lyricae contains his most ambitious literary efforts; in it occurs, for instance, *The Day of Judgment,
an Ode, in English Sapphic.* The first edition contained also four psalm imitations (I in Long Meter, III
in Common Meter, C in Long Meter and CXXXIII
in Common Meter);[31] and a piece entitled "An Hymn

[29] *Ibid.,* p. 156.

[30] Throughout this discussion the name "David" has been used
generically to designate the authors of the Biblical Psalms, in the
same sense in which "Homer" is designated the author of the *Iliad*
and *Odyssey.*

[31] These four Psalm imitations were copied almost exactly from
the 1706 volume into the 1719 volume. As example of the kind of
change Watts made we quote a stanza first from the 1706 volume,
and below it the same stanza from the 1719 volume:

(1706)   p. 61   'Tis like the Oyl on Aaron shed
                 Which choice Perfumes compose,
                 Down softly from his Reverend Head
                 It trickled to his Toes.
(1719)   p. 35   'Tis like the Oyl divinely sweet
                 On Aaron's reverend Head,
                 The trickling Drops perfum'd his Feet,
                 And o'er his Garments spread.

In the actual singing of the last line of this stanza "trickled to his
Toes" lined out alone might have caused some hesitation, or perhaps
merriment.

of Praise to the God of England for Three Great Sal-
vations, I. From the Spanish Invasion, 1588 II. From
the Gunpowder Plot, November 5 III. From Popery
and Slavery by King William of Glorious Memory,
who landed November 5, 1688."

A theme developed with tremolo and harp registra-
tion in his early *Horae Lyricae*, but which his later
considered judgment told him to avoid, was the Divine
Love theme. Though he did not recognize the bathos
of the God of England theme, he at least later had
perspicacity enough to discard the language of physical
rapture he had used in the Divine Love poems of his
1706 volume. Thirty years afterwards he apologized
for the grossness of imagery in these particular poems.
Long before Freud, Watts, a confirmed bachelor, came
to sense the dangers of incorporating expressions of
physical rapture into the poetry addressed to the Almighty.[32]   In 1737 he wrote:

I know it hath been said that this language of rapture addressed to Deity is but a new track given to the flow of the
softer powers, after the disappointment of some meaner
love; or, at least, it is owing to the want of a proper object
and opportunity to fix those tender passions.[33]

John Wesley, who often praised Watts's hymns,
nevertheless could find only words of rebuke when discussing these poems of Divine Love. A friend of his,
Wesley recounted, called the Divine Love poems "too

---

[32] The language of physical rapture occurs frequently in the mys-
tical religious poetry of the preceding century. See, for instance,
Richard Crashaw's *Hymn to the Name and Honour of the Admirable
Saint Teresa.*
[33] Arthur P. Davis, *Isaac Watts* (New York, 1943), p. 177.

amorous, and fitter to be addressed by a lover to his fellow mortal than by a sinner to the most high God."[34]
With this judgment Wesley concurred. Watts, "who
knew Christ after the flesh," according to Wesley, offended "in a more gross manner, than in anything which
was before published in the English tongue."

What pity is it, that those coarse expressions should appear
in many truly spiritual hymns! How often, in the midst of
excellent verse, are lines inserted which disgrace those that
precede and follow.

Wesley assures us that in his own collections of hymns
he has

particularly endeavored, in all the hymns addressed to our
blessed Lord, to avoid every fondling expression, and to
speak as to the most high God. . . . Some will probably
think that I have been over scrupulous [he omitted "Jesus,
Lover of My Soul" from the Methodist Collection on this
very account, even though his brother wrote the hymn].
. . . I never myself either in verse or prose, in praying or
preaching use the word *dear*, "Dear Lord," or "Dear
Saviour". . . . There is no precedent for, or justification of
addressing it ["dear"] to Christ.[35]

Watts liked the term "dear," and within a dozen
pages used such expressions as "my dearest Lord,"[36]
"the dear Man my Saviour,"[37] "the Man I love,"[38]
"Dear Sovereign."[39] Watts's heart dissolved in ecstasy

[34] John Wesley, *The Works of the Rev. John Wesley* (New York,
1856), II, 443.
[35] *Ibid.*, II, 444.
[36] I. Watts, *Horae Lyricae, Poems Chiefly of the Lyric Kind*
(London, 1706), p. 67.
[37] *Ibid.*, p. 70.
[38] *Ibid.*, p. 75.
[39] *Ibid.*, p. 79.

as he contemplated "those sweet Lips, that Heavenly Look," those sweet lips that "seek my kisses and my Love."[40] Christ "stands and prays to clasp me to his Heart."[41] "His lovely Form meets every dream," while "the Passion reigns thro' all my Veins."[42] The amatory strain continued with Watts's imploring Christ to dwell with him: "Dwell there, for ever dwell, my Love; . . . Let me be lost in thine Embrace as Rivers in the Sea; Or Live Eternity of Days to spend them all with Thee."[43] "Still I would lie in those dear Arms Dissolving still among thy Charms," continued Watts, "And as the moments fly, I'de Breathe away successive Souls." Remembering the connotation of the word *die* in eighteenth-century amatory verse, we see Watts dissolving in the dear arms of Christ like the "Billow [that] after Billow rolls to kiss the Shoar, and Dye."[44]

There is also a poem entitled "The Absence of the Beloved," in which Watts gives free flow to "the softer powers," as he called them thirty years later. "Tell me thou Fairest of thy Kind," he asks Christ, "My Love, my All-Divine, Where may this fainting Head reclin'd Relieve such Cares as mine?" He compares his love-sick condition with that of "the Sick'ning Sheep [who] to Coverts fly." The sheep are "not half so scorch't as I thus languishing in Love."[45] In another passage Watts says "the dear Flame is Charming Sweet, I would not cool the Passion yet, Nor can I bear the pain." Between a desire to enjoy the dear flame so

[40] *Ibid.*, p. 80.
[41] *Ibid.*, p. 81.
[42] *Ibid.*, p. 83.
[43] *Ibid.*, p. 84.
[44] *Ibid.*
[45] *Ibid.*, p. 86.

charming sweet and the pain the burning causes, "Strangely I'm Rack't in wide Extremes, I burn, I burn, I burn, and yet I love the Flames." A little later while he is still burning, burning, burning, he asks, "Oh why is Love so strong, and Nature's self so weak?" He pleads with his Christ: "Dear Lord, forgive my rash Complaint and Love me still . . . Unvail thy Beauties tho' I faint."[46] He decides, "I'le carve our Passion on the Bark," and then the "wounded trees" will "drop and bear some Mystick Mark." He continues his pleading, "Look down, Almighty Grace, Prison me round in thine Embrace."[47]

His attitude towards Christ may in large measure have reflected his own belief in the everlasting humanity of Christ. Nowadays in studying his hymns we may perhaps not realize that he entertained peculiar views on the Glorified Humanity of Christ. For the most part, his original ideas on Christ and the Trinity never reached a wide public, and because he became known as a writer of hymns and psalms, his dangerous tracts were conveniently forgotten.

In *The Glory of Christ as God-Man*, Dr. Watts hazarded the opinion that "Michael is Jesus Christ, because he is called . . . the first of the princes, that is, the prime archangel."[48] Watts "confirms this sentiment" that Christ and Michael are the same beings from Revelation 12:7.[49] He continues, "Perhaps this Michael, that is

[46] *Ibid.*, p. 87.   [47] *Ibid.*, p. 92.
[48] I. Watts, *Discourses, Essays, and Tracts, on Various Subjects* (London, 1753), VI, 749.
[49] *Ibid.*, p. 749 ("And there was war in heaven: Michael and his angels fought against the dragon. . . ." Since Christ is head of the host marching against Satan, Watts infers that Michael in this passage must mean Christ.)

Christ the King of the Jews, is the only archangel, or
prince and head of all angels."[50]   A little later he ventures the opinion that "Jesus Christ was that angel who
generally appeared in ancient times to the patriarchs and
to the Jews."[51]

According to Watts, God constantly resided in this
angel (Christ-Michael) and influenced this angel.[52]
God has now given this archangel, or prince and head of
all angels, dominion and power over all things. "This
government of Christ is frequently represented as a
gift and a reward, and therefore must belong eminently
to the inferior nature [of Christ], which alone is capable
of rewards and gifts from God."[53]   It is because God
has exalted Christ to be intercessor that Christ can particularly assist man, and not because Christ can himself
"bestow effectual succour and relief."[54]   In keeping with
the spirit of his century Watts proposes to give "A
rational account how the man Jesus Christ may be
vested with such extensive powers."[55]   Christ, he declares, does not now know "every single thought, word,
or action of every particular creature," but does know
"all the greater, more general, and more considerable
affairs and transactions of nations, churches, and particular persons."[56]   Christ's human soul is "the brightest
image or copy of the divine nature that is found among
mere creatures."[57]   Watts supposes that "it belongs only
to the omniscience of God himself to take in with one
infinite, simultaneous and extensive view all the shapes,
sizes, situations and motions" of every atom of the Uni-

[50] Ibid., p. 749.
[52] Ibid., p. 763.
[54] Ibid., p. 782.
[56] Ibid.
[51] Ibid., p. 752.
[53] Ibid., p. 778.
[55] Ibid., p. 785.
[57] Ibid., p. 786.

verse,[58] and Christ who is "mere creature" does not share this prerogative. Christ, in the analogy of the author, is like a general watching a battle from an elevated position; he knows the way the battle is going, but "cannot know every sword that is drawn, nor hear every groan."[59] Not even the "glorious created mind of Christ" can share the infinite knowledge of God.

Watts, because he thought of Christ as a glorified angel now exalted to the highest dominion in heaven, was once asked why he did not alter some passages in his early hymns in order more exactly to suit them to his matured theological views; his reply is worth quoting:

I freely answer I wish some things were corrected. But . . . I might tell you, that of all the books I have written, that particular copy is not mine. I sold it to Mr. Lawrence near thirty years ago, and his posterity make money of it to this day, and I can scarce claim a right to make any alteration in the book which would alter the sale of it.[60]

John Wesley, whose opinion of Watts's Divine Love poems has been given, threw out a penetrating view on Watts's theology: "Some years since," comments Wesley, "I read about fifty pages of Dr. Watts's ingenious treatise upon the 'Glorified Humanity of Christ.' But it so confounded my intellects, and plunged me into such unprofitable reasons, yea, dangerous ones, that I would not have read it through for five hundred pounds." "It led him [Watts] into Arianism.

[58] *Ibid.*, p. 787.
[59] *Ibid.*
[60] Louis F. Benson, *The Early Editions of Doctor Watts's Hymns* (Philadelphia, 1902), p. 15.

Take care that similar tracts (all of which I abhor) have not the same effect upon you."[61]

At the last, Watts, in one of his more passionate outbursts, found himself still absolutely baffled "and unsatisfied with respect to the God he was to worship."[62] In a paroxysm of despair he cried out, "Surely I ought to know the God whom I worship, whether he be one pure simple being or whether thou art a three-fold deity. . . ." Bewildered and beset with the scourge of temptation "to give up thy word and thy gospel as an unintelligible book, and betake myself to the light of nature and reason," he then prayed:

I entreat, O most merciful Father, that thou wilt not suffer the remnant of my short life to be wasted in such endless wanderings, in quest of thee and thy Son Jesus, as a great part of my past days have been . . .[63]

This was the end of the journey for Watts; at the end it was "De Profundis."

But because he did know how to choose and see his path through the dismal dark daze of organized prejudice against hymn-singing, and because he did work out a cunning and successful attack upon the old-fashioned psalm singing of his age, he is remembered. He was a thinker, a poet, and his combination of learning and poesy has not been frequent enough in Christian history. His poetry won the praise not only of such

[61] John Wesley, *The Works* (New York, 1856), VII, 82.
[62] I. Watts, *The Works* (London, 1753), IV, 641.
[63] *Ibid.*

eighteenth-century critics as Johnson,[64] but has continued to win commendation from such perspicacious critics in this century as A. E. Housman (who rated him above Pope, in a fine frenzy of excitement, no doubt)[65] and George Saintsbury, who did not rate him above Pope, but urbanely decided him to be still "really worth reading."

Watts has often been praised for qualifications he never possessed, but while greater figures have been forgotten, he at least bequeathed us some of the noblest hymns in the language.[66]   And now in a day when above all else Christian unity is desired, his hymns have become symbols of a oneness of spirit that may in time transcend every barrier.

[64] Dr. Johnson claimed no acquaintance with Watts's prose. "Of his life I know very little," he said on occasion. Southey was perhaps the first literary critic who gave any attention to Watts's theological opinions. See Johnson, *Lives of the English Poets* (Oxford, 1905), III, 302.

[65] A. E. Housman, *The Name and Nature of Poetry* (Cambridge, 1933), p. 30.

[66] Matthew Arnold called "When I Survey the Wondrous Cross" the greatest. "Our God, Our Help in Ages Past" is also universally recognized as one of the two or three finest hymns in the English tongue.

IX. JOHN WESLEY'S FIRST HYMNBOOK

LONG BEFORE ALDERSGATE—IN FACT, more than thirteen years before his heart was "strangely warmed" — John Wesley began an intimate record of his day-by-day and hour-by-hour spiritual experiences, which for more than a century after his death remained unpublished. During our own century the breaking of the cipher in which the Diaries were written gave access at last to the detailed secrets of those early formative years at Oxford and of those later difficult months in Georgia which preceded the celebrated event of May 24, 1738, when he found himself ushered into a new dimension of spiritual experience.

These Diaries, then, cover a period of greatest significance—the dozen or so years before Aldersgate, and they continue to supply us information for the period lasting until August, 1741, three years after Aldersgate, and two years after his debut as field preacher at Bristol, where he had "submitted to be more vile, and proclaimed in the highways the glad tidings of salvation." If that Aldersgate experience in his thirty-fifth year was indeed the watershed, undoubtedly then the whole tenor of his spiritual life must have changed after May 24, 1738.

And yet, did it really change as drastically as the classical theory of the Aldersgate conversion might imply? True, he may have broken with the nonjuror William Law after 1738 (although the letter precipitat-

ing the rupture was, interestingly enough, written ten
days before, rather than after Aldersgate),[1] and he may
later have told a select company on Sunday, May 28,
"that five days before he was not a Christian,"[2] but,
nevertheless, his day-by-day and hour-by-hour spiritual
routine both before and after May 24 exhibits strange
likenesses.   Dr. Umphrey Lee has by no means been
the only Methodist historian who has regarded "May
24 as in no sense a *terminus ad quem* and *terminus a
quo* of Methodist tradition."[3]

A significant likeness in spiritual routine both before
and after Aldersgate, as revealed in the Diaries, for
instance, is Wesley's uniform devotion to the singing of
psalms and hymns as a daily and even hourly part of his
own spiritual life.   Long before Aldersgate Wesley was
a "singing" man.   Those who have equated his spiritual
condition before Aldersgate with some such state as *The
Dark Night of the Soul* might well remember that in
the Diaries both before and after 1738 "with the exception of 'prayer' and 'conversation' no word appears more
frequently than 'singing'."[4]   Certainly long before he
stood up in company witnessing that he had been no
Christian before May 24, 1738, his had been a singing
religion.

Even more to the point, however, than the mere fact
that Wesley practiced singing four or five times a day
some kind of religious song, both before and after

---

[1] John Wesley, *The Journal of the Rev. John Wesley, A.M.,* . . .
ed. Nehemiah Curnock (London, 1909-1916), VIII, 319-320.
[2] Umphrey Lee, *The Lord's Horseman* (New York, 1928), p. 73.
[3] J. Ernest Rattenbury, *The Conversion of the Wesleys* (London,
1938), p. 118.
[4] John Wesley, *Journal*, II, 72.

Aldersgate, invariably including singing as an integral part of every group meeting, is the fact that he was still continuing to sing the same repertory of hymns at at the close of his ministry that he had selected for the use of his slender congregations in the isolated settlements of Georgia during his legalistic days. His *Collection of Psalms and Hymns* (1738), and again his *Collection of Psalms and Hymns* issued in 1741, in large measure duplicated the choices for his first *Collection of Psalms and Hymns*, printed at Charleston, South Carolina, in 1737. But more remarkable, forty years later when in co-operation with his brother Charles he issued the last collection for specific use in the Methodist Societies, he largely reverted to the very hymns he had chosen for his first hymnbook, the one issued at Charleston in 1737. Surely if he had moved so far from his original moorings as some would have us believe, he would not then have returned in his last *Collection of Psalms and Hymns*, issued in 1784 in London, to those same psalms and hymns that had nourished his spiritual life during the parched years when he was yet wandering about in goatskins, being spiritually destitute, afflicted, and tormented amidst the wilds of Georgia.

What are the precise facts regarding the number of hymns carried over from the *Charlestown Collection* (as the collection is known today—Charleston being then Charlestown) into the last *Collection of Psalms and Hymns* published in 1784? Fortunately for purposes of comparison, the number of items in both collections is not too disparate. The 1737 collection has 70 items (we do not count as individual items the parts of those psalms and hymns which were divided by Wesley into shorter units for convenience in singing); and the 1784 collection (following the same method of counting) has 89 items. Of the 70 items in the *Charlestown Collection*, considerably more than a third, or 27 items, to be exact, were carried over into the collection published by the brothers at the very end of their ventures in collaboration. And it was this 1784 collection which then became later the nucleus of *The Morning Hymn Book*, an enlargement made by Dr. Coke, "and used in London and elsewhere at the forenoon service."[5]

When the 1784 *Collection of Psalms and Hymns* finally did appear we may surmise that John Wesley was in very much the same mood which prompted him later in life to recant some of the misleading statements which had appeared in his early Journals. If he had at one time asserted that he was a "child of wrath" in Georgia, he later wrote in a correction of this and other similarly enthusiastic condemnations of his Georgia spiritual estate, "I believe not."[6] He can hardly have believed he was a "child of wrath" in Georgia when he compiled his 1784 collection (in which he used the same hymns which he had used in his 1737 collection). Recalling the Georgia years, Wesley in 1784 wrote: "The first rise of Methodism, so called, was in November, 1729, when four of us met together at Oxford; the second was at Savannah, in April, 1736." The date May 24, 1738, does not figure in the three stages marking the growth of Methodism; the third date Wesley supplied for the unfolding of the Methodist movement

[5] Richard Green, *The Works of John and Charles Wesley, A Bibliography* (London, 1896), p. 225.

[6] Wesley, *Journal*, I. 423.

significantly antedated Aldersgate. The last stage, Wesley stated in 1781, was reached in 1738, on May 1, "at London . . . when forty or fifty of us agreed to meet together every Wednesday evening, in order to a free conversation, begun and ended with singing and prayer."

Those are the key words, then: every meeting "begun and ended with singing and prayer." This constantly renewed warming of the heart in "singing and prayer," at least as far as the singing was concerned, became possible only because Wesley struck out on an entirely new line when he compiled his first hymnbook and issued it at Charleston.

Before the *Charlestown Collection* of 1737 there were no hymnbooks designed specifically for use in Church of England congregations. A modern scholar has justly called "this little book of seventy hymns . . . the first real Anglican Hymnal."[7] Singing as such was not new in Church of England congregations in 1737, but the singing of hymns was an innovation. The permitted songs were metrical versions of the Davidic Psalms in either the Sternhold and Hopkins Version compiled during the reign of Edward VI or the Tate and Brady Version compiled during the reign of William III. The singing of hymns as such came then as an innovation in the Church of England during the eighteenth century, and not until the early years of the nineteenth century did hymn singing obtain any general vogue; as late as 1819 a lengthy and now famous lawsuit was instigated against a clergyman who at-

[7] Winfred Douglas, *Church Music in History and Practice* (New York, 1937), p. 235.

tempted to "introduce into his parish church a book containing . . . hymns." And for more than a hundred years after John Wesley's epochal hymnbook "bishops continued to issue formal charges to their dioceses against the introduction of hymns into parochial worship."

Wesley had no bishop at hand in Georgia to protest the innovation of hymn singing, but he did encounter a layman, Thomas Causton (uncle of the eighteen-year-old girl whom he for a while courted), who protested. At the end of August, 1737, he was haled before a Grand Jury to hear a list of grievances in the following order. First, "inverting the order and method of the Liturgy." Second, "changing . . . the version of Psalms publicly authorized to be sung in the church." Third, "introducing into the church and service at the Altar compositions of psalms and hymns not inspected or authorized by any proper judicature."[8] There can be little doubt that Wesley was guilty on all three counts.

During his sojourn in Georgia he used as a manual of devotions George Hickes's *Reformed Devotions,* a manual compiled from an English Roman Catholic, John Austin. George Hickes had himself become a nonjuring bishop, and had late in life (during Queen Anne's reign) returned to London with an overflow of enthusiasm for the first Edwardine Prayerbook. During his Georgia ministry Wesley used Hickes along with Thomas à Kempis and the Psalter for his daily devotional exercises.[9] The Diaries contain numerous references to Hickes who, of course, had provided in the

[8] Wesley, *Journal,* I, 385.
[9] *Ibid.,* I, 122.

Devotions suitable collects, scripture readings, and hymns for the principal hours of the day "in the Antient Way of Offices," that is to say, after the ancient pattern of monastic offices.[10] Both John and Charles followed Hickes and the nonjurors in preferring the 1549 Edwardine Prayerbook, "because they believed it to be more in harmony with the usage of the early church than any other, as undoubtedly it is."[11] Causton and his crowd were therefore right when they accused Wesley of "inverting the order and method of the Liturgy." Those who adhered to the 1662 prayer book would necessarily have found Wesley's use of the 1549 prayer book captious and irritating.

Wesley took from Hickes seven hymns printed in the *Collection of Psalms and Hymns* at Charleston in 1737. Hickes, in turn, had derived his hymns from Austin, a convert to Rome whose hymns, thirty-nine in number, published at Paris during the early Restoration period (1668), exerted an influence far beyond the bounds of the Roman communion.[12] Hickes usually printed more stanzas in his *Reformed Devotions* than Wesley found space for in his own *Charlestown Collection;* but aside from being abbreviated, Hickes's hymns were scarcely touched by Wesley. In conformity with his own dislike for "fondling expressions" addressed to Deity, Wesley did change the first word of a hymn

[10] *Ibid.*, I, 187, 201, 218, 267-269, 285, 295, 299, 307, 315, 347.

[11] *Ibid.*, I, 210. On Sunday, May 9, 1736, John Wesley stated in his *Journal:* "I began dividing the public prayers, according to the original appointment of the Church." He followed those nonjurors such as Hickes who always celebrated according to 1549 usage.

[12] Louis F. Benson, *The English Hymn* (Philadelphia, 1915), p. 69.

entitled "Inconstancy" to read: "*Lord* Jesu, when, when, shall it be,"[13] whereas both John Austin and George Hickes have "Dear Jesu, when, when shall it be."[14]   He also changed a word in Hymn XXXVIII entitled "Hymn to Christ." Hickes, following Austin, had written "Sweet Jesu, why, why dost thou Love";[15] Wesley gave the following first line: "*O* Jesu, why, why dost thou Love."[16]   Perhaps the most beautiful of Austin's hymns preserved by John Wesley was

> Come, Holy Spirit, send down those beams
> Which gently flow in silent streams
> From the eternal throne above. . . .[17]

This hymn again appears in the last *Collection of Psalms and Hymns,* published at London in 1784.[18] Another fine one from Austin is the Christmas hymn found in the 1737 collection, "Jesu, Behold the Wise from Far."[19]

The second charge drawn up against Wesley by the

[13] Wesley, *Collection of Psalms and Hymns* (Charles-Town [Charleston, S. C.], 1737), p. 55.

[14] George Hickes, *Devotions in the Antient Way of Offices, Reform'd by a Person of Quality* (London, 1846; reprint of 5th ed., 1717), p. 36.

[15] *Ibid.,* p. 266.

[16] Wesley, *Collection,* 1737, p. 36.

[17] *Ibid.,* p. 22; Hickes, p. 316.

[18] *Collection,* 1784, p. 32. The original in John Austin, *Devotions in the Antient Way of Offices* (4th ed., 1685), p. 412. The seven hymns from Austin in the 1737 collection are: Hymns XVII (Austin, p. 363, Hickes, p. 278), XXII (Austin, p. 412, Hickes, p. 316), XXIV (Austin, p. 4, Hickes, p. 3), XXXIV (Austin, p. 493, Hickes, p. 351), XXXVIII (Austin, p. 349, Hickes, p. 266), LVIII (Austin, p. 52, Hickes, p. 36), LXVIII (Austin, p. 86, Hickes, p. 59). None of the earliest Wesley collections was provided with index, nor do Austin or Hickes have indices.

[19] *Collection,* 1737, p. 18.

Grand Jury read: "changing . . . the version of Psalms publicly authorized to be sung in the church." The two versions of metrical psalms authorized in the Church of England were the Sternhold and Hopkins Version and the Tate and Brady Version. The Tate and Brady Version, published in 1696, had been especially commended by Wesley's immediate ecclesiastical superior, under whose loose supervision all religious life in the colonies was organized, the Bishop of London. Shortly after it appeared the Bishop of London had "heartily recommended the Use of this Version to all his Brethren within his Diocese,"[20] Wesley certainly knew the Tate and Brady. During the voyage to Georgia he used it,[21] but evidently he found it excessively florid. The Diaries show him studying it again later for possible use,[22] but when he came to the actual printing of the *Charlestown Collection* he preferred to use psalms taken from Isaac Watts's 1719 volume, rather than from Tate and Brady. Fourteen "psalms" in Wesley's 1737 collection are derived from Watts; another four are metrical versions taken from a devotional manual published by Samuel Wesley, John Wesley's father, entitled, *The Pious Communicant Rightly Prepared.*

Of the remaining "psalms" included in the *Charlestown Collection,* one was by "a gentlman of Exeter College," a student friend of the Wesleys, Thomas Broughton by name;[23] another (Psalm CIV, a favorite

[20] L. F. Benson, *The English Hymn* (Philadelphia, 1915), p. 48.

[21] Wesley, *Journal,* I, 123. Subsequent uses of Tate and Brady, pp. 184 and 302.

[22] *Ibid.,* p. 175 (Diary, March 5, 1736).

[23] *Ibid.,* p. 456. For a transcription of this "psalm" in its earliest form, see John Telford, *The Letters of the Rev. John Wesley, A.M.* (London, 1931), I, 31. Wesley copied nine verses of Broughton's paraphrase in his letter of April 4, 1726, to his brother, Samuel.

of Wesley, translated by him during his Oxford days[24] but in a version which he never used in any of his collections intended for congregational singing) has been attributed, but incorrectly, to George Sandys;[25] and still another, Psalm XIX, is the famous version by Joseph Addison, "The Spacious Firmament on High." But where were the authorized versions of metrical psalms? The colonists had it right when they complained that Wesley had changed the "version of Psalms publicly authorized to be sung in the church."

If he neglected Tate and Brady, at least he did choose psalm versions which even now retain their popularity. Addison's "The Spacious Firmament on High" has reappeared in innumerable hymnals, usually with the music of "The Heavens are Telling" (from Haydn's oratorio, *The Creation*). Another psalm-rendering found in the 1737 collection which retains its popularity today is that one by Watts beginning, "Come Ye that Love the Lord." Still another which has retained its hold on the affections of the public is Watts's version of Psalm C, "Before Jehovah's Awful [or as it is spelled in the Methodist Hymnal, *awe-full*] Throne." A fourth "psalm" found in the 1737 collection which is still included in the present Methodist Hymnal—and with a tune, surprisingly enough, included by Wesley in the first Methodist tunebook of 1742[26]—is Watts' his-

[24] Thomas W. Herbert, *John Wesley as Editor and Author* (Princeton, N. J., 1940), p. 48.

[25] John and Charles Wesley, *The Poetical Works*, collected and arranged by G. Osborn (London, 1869), II, 6, line 20.

[26] *Collection of Tunes Set to Music as they are commonly sung at the Foundery* (London, 1742), p. 35. The words associated with this tune in the 1742 collection, however, are those of Samuel Wesley, "Ye Priests of God whose Happy Days" (a paraphrase of Psalm CXIII), the text of which appeared in the 1737 *Charlestown Collection*, p. 6.

torically important rendering of Psalm CXLVI, "I'll Praise My Maker While I've Breath."

This last psalm version was Wesley's own dying favorite. The general impression has been that he died with the words on his lips: "The best of all is, God is with us." But the record shows that on Tuesday, March 1, 1791, he "broke out in a manner which, considering his extreme weakness astonished us all, in these blessed words:

> I'll praise my Maker while I've breath
> And when my voice is lost in death,
> Praise shall employ my nobler powers;
> My days of praise shall ne'er be past,
> While life, and thought, and being last,
> Or immortality endures."

The account continues, showing that the next day when he died, those words, "I'll praise—I'll praise—!" were the last before "Farewell." One writer who spent Tuesday night with the eighty-eight-year-old Wesley before his death reported that "Wesley repeated 'I'll praise' at least some scores of times" during the night.[27] Those far-off days in Georgia must have seemed not so far off, but very near when Wesley at the end returned to those very hymns, or "psalms," which had formed the nucleus of the 1737 collection. Space and time were then annihilated at the end, when he returned to that confident assertion he had made at the very inception of his ministry, during the Georgia days: "My days of praise shall ne'er be past, While life, and thought, and being last, Or immortality endures."

[27] Wesley, *Journal*, VIII, 143.

The third charge which the Georgia colonists brought against him was that of "introducing into the church . . . hymns not inspected or authorized by any proper judicature." Austin's hymns certainly had not been inspected or authorized by any proper judicature. Hickes, who collected them, was a most improper person from every Established Church point of view. And what of the other authors of hymns included in the 1737 collection? Watts labored under the difficulty of being a Dissenter; the days were not too remote when Watts's own father had been imprisoned for his dissenting views. Even Dr. Johnson, admirer of Watts's piety, could not forgive Watts for his Dissent.[28]

But thoroughly respectable from an Established point of view should have been another upon whom Wesley drew copiously for his 1737 collection, and upon whom he continued to draw intensively for his later collections—George Herbert. Herbert, author of *The Temple,* was an Anglican of unblemished virtue, a model parish priest, an Anglican Curé of Ars, if one will have it that way. His poetry, published posthumously, shares the virtues inherent in other poetry of the metaphysical seventeenth-century group. During the eighteenth century, Wesley (who had learned his Herbert at Epworth, where Susannah Wesley had read *The Temple* to her children)[29] was almost alone in keeping alive the memory and reputation of Herbert. Of the six Herbert hymns in the 1737 collection all have been radically altered from their source, in order to fit them

[28] Samuel Johnson, *Lives of the English Poets* (Oxford, 1905), III, 311. "Happy will be that reader who imitates Watts in all but his non-conformity."

[29] J. A. Leger, *La Jeunesse de Wesley* (Paris, 1910), pp. 14, 20.

for congregational usage. Perhaps most interesting on account of changes related to doctrinal interests is Hymn XLIX, "A Sinner's Prayer," beginning "Thou Lord my Power and Wisdom art."[30]

Charles Wesley had not yet found his creative muse when he accompanied John on the Georgia trip. More helpful at this stage was another brother, Samuel Wesley, headmaster of a school in England, who gave the paten and chalice used in the church at Savannah.[31] Five hymns by this other brother were included in the 1737 collection, and all five of these reappear in the 1784 collection.

The last group of hymns were Wesley's translations from the German; he included five in the 1737 collection. John Wesley was one of the very few University men of his generation with any real knowledge of German.[32] Almost two centuries before Wesley's *Charlestown Collection*, Miles Coverdale had issued in 1539 the first collection incorporating translations from the German. Contemporaneously with Coverdale, a Scottish pair, the Wedderburn brothers, had issued a volume of *Gude and Godlie Ballates* which also drew heavily upon German sources. But after the Wedderburns in Scotland, and Coverdale with his *Goostly Psalmes and Spirituall Songes* in England, the interest in German hymns had died.

Wesley providentially was thrown into company with the Moravians aboard ship on his voyage out, and immediately began the study of German; that he actually

---

[30] *Collection*, 1737, p. 47.

[31] Wesley, *Journal*, I, 213.

[32] James T. Hatfield, "John Wesley's Translations of German Hymns," *PMLA*, XI (1896), 185.

mastered it has been proved by the late Professor
Hatfield of Northwestern University, who after analysis
stated that Wesley's knowledge of the tongue was in
some respects superior to that of Scott and Coleridge in
the next century. In all, Wesley translated thirty-three
German hymns, most of them while still in Georgia.
Among these was the translation from the German mystic, Tersteegen, which in its translated form Emerson
termed the "greatest hymn" in the English language.[33]
Of the five in the 1737 collection, one was by Count
Zinzendorf, spiritual leader of the Moravians, and the
remaining four by intimates of A. H. Francke, spiritual
leader of the Halle Pietists. The five German hymns
first published in the 1737 collection, and also the others
translated in Georgia but first published after his return
to England, were frequently reprinted. As late as
1780, "O God, Thou Bottomless Abyss," the same
hymn as number XVI in the 1737 collection, found its
way almost unaltered into the most famous of his large
collections.

Fortunately for the history of hymn-singing, Wesley
was thrown into contact not with the Salzburgers, but
rather with the Moravians during his journey to
America. The Moravians were baptized by episcopally
ordained ministers; the Salzburgers, another dissident
group amongst the Georgia colonists, were not. Wesley
could commune with the Moravians; by act of Parliament in 1749 the Moravians *(Unitas Fratrum)* were
acknowledged "an ancient Episcopal Church." Their
bishops were accounted members of the apostolic suc-

[33] Henry Bett, *The Hymns of Methodism* (3rd ed.; London,
1945), p. 13.

cession; Wesley was in no sense denying his own convictions when he associated with them in religious enterprise and learned German in order to translate their favorite hymns.

During Wesley's sojourn in Georgia there was no separate building set apart as a chapel—the chapel was usually a room in the courthouse.[34] But there were books, some of them supplied by Dr. Bray's Associates (who sent books to S. P. G. missionaries), some of them Wesley's own books, and some of them books borrowed from the Germans; from these he was able to compile the epoch-making *Charlestown Collection*.

The actual process of publication may be briefly summarized. The printer was Lewis Timothy, a Huguenot immigrant who came to Charleston by way of Philadelphia. Benjamin Franklin set him up in the printing business in South Carolina with a six-year partnership contract which was to run from 1733 until 1739.[35] Timothy died before the expiration of the contract period, and his son Peter was left later to take over the business. Lewis Timothy had been for a time librarian of the Philadelphia Library Society (1732) and Franklin spoke of him as "a man of learning."[36] His was undoubtedly a spirit which Wesley found congenial on his first trip to Charleston in August of 1736. Probably it was on Tuesday, August 3, that Wesley met Timothy and discussed the printing of the collection. This first visit to Charleston lasted only a week, but Wesley returned again the following April for a second visit last-

[34] Wesley, *Journal*, I, 213.
[35] Douglas C. McMurtrie, *A History of Printing in the United States* (New York, 1936), II, 315.
[36] *Ibid.*, p. 320.

ing ten days. This second visit was made in order to "stop the proceedings of one in Carolina, who had married several of my parishioners without either banns or licence," but he also looked after his publishing interests while there. The day of his arrival in Charleston for his second visit he immediately went to Timothy, and spent from eight in the morning until half-past nine discussing the printing of the collection.[37] This meeting was on Thursday, and Wesley saw Timothy again the next Tuesday at nine in the morning. The third and last visit to Charleston occurred in December of the same year, 1737, during Wesley's passage back to England.

Timothy published a weekly newspaper, the *South-Carolina Gazette*, but not until 1740 did an advertisement of Wesley's collection of hymns appear. On March 8, 1740, after the flurry of excitement caused by George Whitefield's visit to the colonies, the following notice appeared in the *Gazette:* "To be sold by the Printer hereof, Price 5 s. A choice Collection of Psalms and Hymns, By the Rev. Mr. Wesley, Itinerant Preacher in England and Predecessor to the Rev. Mr. Whitefield."[38] Two items in the advertisement are noteworthy—first, the price, which seems higher than the prices asked for later hymnbooks Wesley published in England: Carolina currency was, of course, inflated;

[37] Wesley, *Journal*, I. 347. It seems that Wesley placed the hymns in Timothy's hands for printing during the first Charleston visit; during the second Charleston visit the sheets were ready for his proofreading. He mentioned correcting proof at nine in the evening, April 18, 1737.

[38] D. C. McMurtrie, "A Bibliography of South Carolina Imprints, 1731-1740," *South Carolina Historical and Genealogical Magazine*, XXXIV (July, 1933), 132.

secondly, the connection with Whitefield. Whitefield's
"Letter vindicating his having asserted that Archbishop
Tillotson knew no more of Christianity than Mahomet"
had appeared under the imprint of Peter Timothy that
same year, and the colony was astir with religious excitement. Whitefield, arrested by warrant from the
Chief Justice, had written a letter (which Peter
Timothy published) asserting "the clergy of South
Carolina broke their canons daily."[39] Whitefield's name
had risen into a sort of meteoric prominence during this
excitement; undoubtedly Wesley's 1737 volume was
thrust just at this time into the public eye with the
hope of reaping a belated profit. Whitefield's name was
used, as it were, to advertise Wesley.

The exact nature of Wesley's financial dealings with
Timothy, however, remains obscure. Franklin had already complained that Lewis Timothy, the father, "was
ignorant in matters of account," and we are unable now
to reconstruct the precise financial agreement between
Wesley and Timothy. Wesley must have paid the
initial printing costs. There is an interesting letter to
the Georgia Trustees, written March 4, 1737, in which
Wesley in unforeseen vein laments the sharp curtail-
ment of "mission appropriations." Wesley undoubtedly needed more money in Georgia than the S. P. G.
provided.

Timothy's only previous excursion into the printing
of religious matter was the publication of a sermon by a
Congregationalist minister in South Carolina, issued the

[39] Isaiah Thomas, *The History of Printing in America* (2nd ed.;
Albany, 1874), I, 342.

year before Wesley's collection.[40]   The sermon, printed
in larger type, occupied twenty-six pages; Wesley's collection, published with a considerable number of misprints, if he actually "corrected proof" as has been assumed, was in smaller type, occupying seventy-four
pages, and appeared on a quality of paper that has with-
stood the rigors of time and use in a distinguished manner.   The only copy of the 1737 *Charlestown Collection*
still extant in the United States is deposited in the
Lenox Collection of the New York Public Library.
What appears to be the only other known copy is in
England; it is also of interest here to note that only
three copies of the 1738 volume, *A Collection of Psalms
and Hymns,* survive.

Detailed study of the 1737 collection has indicated
that Wesley even during the "Cimmerian darkness" of
his Georgia period had already developed a basic technique in the use of hymns which he did not alter later in
life.   At journey's end he was still thinking in very
much the same religious categories which occupied him
at the time he compiled his Georgia hymnal.   The 1784
collection and the 1737 collection because of their
astounding likeness prove Wesley's loyalty even in old
age to the religious insights of the Georgia days.

But even more significant than his continued loyalty
to his Georgia methods was his merit in pioneering there
with the first Anglican hymnal.   And if it was the first
Anglican hymnal it was also a Methodist hymnal.   His
was indeed the basic part in shaping Methodist hym-

[40] Whitmarsh, Timothy's predecessor at Charleston, had printed a
Visitation Sermon in 1733.   Printing began in South Carolina in
1731.

nody, the crowning glory of the Methodist movement. His brother's "right Promethean fire" has sometimes deflected the student from a too exacting analysis of John Wesley's part—but John Wesley was the instigator and, throughout, the controlling influence in the outburst of evangelical song.

At the end it was not "Jesus, Lover of My Soul," beautiful though we may find that hymn, nor was it any other Charles Wesley hymn that we prize today which haunted him, but rather a hymn he had selected and revised in Georgia. Wesley, who continues to dominate evangelical thought, exerts his influence in the *methods* which he chose and perfected for the spread of evangelical religion. Chief among his methods was hymn-singing. In the light of subsequent development, the *Charlestown Collection* assumes hitherto unrecognized importance.

X. THE MUSICAL WESLEYS

THE FLOWERING OF MUSICAL GENIUS IN THE WESLEY FAMILY OF THE SECOND AND THIRD GENERATIONS

CHARLES WESLEY, THE HYMN WRIT-
er, had two sons, both of whom possessed truly
extraordinary gifts in music. Dr. William
Boyce, the Nestor of eighteenth-century musicians,
compared the younger of them with Wolfgang
Amadeus Mozart,[1] and probably did not exaggerate unduly. At an early age these two sons of the hymn
writer were performing regularly in concert before such
notables as the Lord Mayor of London and the Archbishop of Canterbury. After his sojourn in Bristol the
elder Charles Wesley brought his two sons to London
in order better to exhibit their talents.[2] He wrote his
brother, John Wesley, telling with pride of the profits
and success of the fashionable concerts which his two
sons were giving in their fine town house at Marylebone. (Charles Wesley retained throughout life a hankering after aristocracy. Near the end of his life he
wrote for the edification of one of his sons: "You must

[1] James T. Lightwood, *Samuel Wesley, Musician* (London, 1937), p. 22.
[2] *Ibid.*, p. 48. "In his eager desire to parade his sons' talents, and obtain influential interest for them, [Charles Wesley] seems to have penetrated into somewhat unlikely quarters." He wrote, for instance, to such persons as Dr. Hayes, Professor of Music at Oxford, and Edward Walpole, son of George II's Prime Minister, notables whom he had never met, in an endeavor to intrude his sons into public notice.

be content to be a gentleman only, such as you are born."³)

With a pardonable excess of paternal pride he tried to convince his brother, John Wesley, that the finger of the Lord was apparent in the musical adventures of his two sons. John Wesley wrote back his opinion that the hand of the Lord was *not* in the musical adventures of his precocious nephews. Upon Charles's insistence he did consent to deck himself in full canonicals on one or two occasions in order to cut a proper figure at their fashionable concerts. John Wesley, however, expressed the kind of reaction one might expect when he recorded in his *Journal,* after one of the affairs, his own preference for plain people:

January 25, 1781. . . . I spent an agreeable hour at a concert at my nephews, but I was a little out of my element among lords and ladies. I love plain music and plain company best.⁴

The names of the two sons of the hymn writer were Charles and Samuel. These two names recur so often in Wesley family annals that confusion easily arises. Without attempting to unravel the tangled web of family relations, the names of the more important musical

³ *Ibid.,* p. 47.
⁴ John Wesley, *The Journal of the Rev. John Wesley, A.M.* . . . ed. Nehemiah Curnock (London, 1915), VI, 303. Among the guests on this occasion was General Oglethorpe, founder of the Georgia Colony, now more than eighty years old, who had come to hear the sons of his old secretary (Charles Wesley, the hymn writer, had served Oglethorpe, not too satisfactorily, in Georgia, 1736). At this musical party Oglethorpe "met John Wesley and kissed his hand in token of respect." Also present at this historic occasion is thought to have been (among other nobility) the father of the Duke of Wellington.

geniuses of the family may be stated immediately. Charles (born 1757) and Samuel (born 1766) and Samuel Sebastian (born 1810) all showed extraordinary ability. Samuel Wesley was the foremost English composer of church music during his lifetime, and his natural son, Samuel Sebastian Wesley, inheriting the mantle of his father, attained high academic distinction (D. Mus. from Oxford) and a lasting reputation in the larger world of nineteenth-century musical history. Concerning their contributions to the musical repertory, Dannreuther, in the *Oxford History of Music*, says:

In the musical history of the nineteenth century the work of the two Wesleys [Samuel and Samuel Sebastian] is of real importance. . . . They tower above their English contemporaries, laymen or churchmen.[5]

Both Charles and Samuel, sons of the hymn writer, suffered from the unreasoned dislike in Established Church circles for the Wesley name. Though universally accorded recognition as a superlative organist, Charles, rebuffed in an attempt to secure an important organ position, heard the remark: "We want no Wesleys here!"[6] Even King George III's appreciative recognition of his talents never obtained for him a position as organist in the Established Church commensurate with his abilities. Samuel, his younger brother, suffered the same fate, but even more unjustly. To add mischief to his lot, even the Wesleyan Methodists treated him with undisguised impatience. On one occasion while visiting Cambridge Samuel came across settings of hymns writ-

[5] Edward Dannreuther, *The Oxford History of Music*, [1905], VI, 289.
[6] Lightwood, *op. cit.*, p. 228.

ten by his father. The music was written, appropriately enough, by the acknowledged darling of the English musical public, George Frederick Handel. Samuel Wesley sent the hymns with the music in score to the Wesleyan Methodist printer; but despite his pains in unearthing and editing the hymns he never received a cordial response from the Wesleyans, and in fact had difficulty collecting a small pittance from a rather sizable profit realized on the sale of the hymns.[7]

The Wesleyans as well as the Established Church party had good reason to suspect the religious sincerity of the younger of John Wesley's nightingale nephews. The official religious connection of Samuel Wesley was a scandal in his youth. Attracted by the pleasing liturgy at the Portuguese Chapel (he later said "the Gregorian music had seduced him"), Samuel embraced the Roman Catholic faith in 1784 (his age was then eighteen). His father found out the whole affair in due time, and we may surmise that he began to doubt the finger of the Lord in his son's musical vagaries. John Wesley, upon learning the tenor of events, wrote an expostulatory letter to his nephew, but the damage had been done.[8]

[7] *Ibid.*, p. 197. None of these three tunes (*Gopsal, Cannons,* and *Fitzwilliam*) has achieved the popularity that the factitious Handel tune, not really a Handel tune at all—but in "Handel's style"— "Joy to the World," has attained. "Great composers" have rarely been successful in writing popular hymn tunes.

[8] John Wesley, *The Letters* . . . , ed. John Telford (London, 1931), VII, 231. "Whether of this Church or that I care not; you can be saved in either, or damned in either. . . . Whether Bellarmine or Luther be right, you are certainly wrong if you are not born of the Spirit." This first letter to Samuel from his "affectionate Uncle" was followed by yet another letter (*Letters*, VIII, 218) in which with considerable tact for a man of eighty-seven John Wesley said: "I fear you want (what you least of all suspect) . . .

Samuel celebrated his entrance into the Roman Catholic Church with a mass dedicated to Pius VI, the reigning pope. His dedication, written in atrocious Latin, was acknowledged by His Holiness in a communication sent though the intermediacy of the Apostolic Delegate; in it the Pope said weak minds were attracted by music, but he also expressed the pious hope that Samuel might not limit his future service to the writing of music, but might engage himself more actively as disputant in theological matters. Samuel, however, turned out to be a sore disappointment to his Catholic friends. He soon fell away from the Catholic Church, although he preserved a life-long interest in Gregorian chant and continued on the friendliest of terms with the organist at the Portuguese Chapel, Vincent Novello, founder of the famous British publishing firm.[9]

the religion of the heart; the religion which Kempis, Pascal, Fenelon enjoyed." Commenting on this letter from which we have just quoted, Umphrey Lee (*John Wesley and Modern Religion*, [Nashville, 1936], p. 144) calls it "One of the most beautiful letters which John Wesley ever wrote."

[9] In 1819 when Samuel Wesley was reduced to penury Vincent Novello was his last resource of hope. Novello left the note from his friend, Samuel, asking for a position as copyist, with the following endorsement: "I wish to place this affecting note on record, as an eternal disgrace to the pretended patrons of good music in England, who could have the contemptible bad taste to undervalue and neglect the masterly productions of such an extraordinary musician as Sam Wesley . . . a real genius (who like Purcell, was an honour to the country where he was born)." Novello lashed out then at the "undeserved neglect" which had forced Wesley to "seek employment as a mere drudging *Copyist* to prevent himself from starvation." Novello added this indictment: "The behaviour of the *rich Patrons* of Wesley in *England* reminds me of the equally despicable behaviour of the self-styled nobility among the cold-blooded, selfish, and beggarly-proud Scotch towards their really illustrious countryman, *Burns*."

Not the least surprising thing about the career of Samuel Wesley was his proleptic espousal of opinions now held in informed circles not only on the values of Gregorian chant but also upon the supreme worth of the music of J. S. Bach. Samuel Wesley expressed his fanatical attachment to the music of J. S. Bach in a number of interesting ways. His son bore the name Sebastian in tribute to The Man, as he liked to refer to the Great Johann Sebastian. Early nineteenth-century England was still under the tenacious spell of Handel. The greatness of Bach went unrecognized by even so learned an authority as Charles Burney. Samuel Wesley started a one-man crusade in behalf of Bach, assisting in the first usable edition of the *Well-Tempered Clavier* published in England, and playing in season and out of season, for audiences at times obtuse, the masterpieces of The Man. In our own day, when Bach's music has attained universal recognition and when Gregorian chant receives ever wider appreciation, Samuel Wesley's musical taste seems nothing short of a hundred years in advance of his epoch.

Despite the considerable self-satisfaction that Samuel Wesley must have drawn from his own composition (recognized as the best English creative work of the early nineteenth century) he came in later life bitterly to regret his choice of a career. In a letter to his mother (1806) written in his fortieth year he said:

I have every day more cause to curse the day that ever my poor father suffered *musick* to be my profession. In this country experience continually shows that only impudent and ignorant wretches make any considerable emolument by it

. . . but the whole is a degrading business to any man of spirit or any abilities.[10]

In the same letter he says he would open a gin shop if he had sufficient capital, since only in that direction does he see any hope of making money. Charles Wesley, his father, could hardly have approved of the gin business, but it is certain that he would have approved even less of his son's extramarital relations. Samuel's unapproved relation resulted in the birth of his famous son, Samuel Sebastian, perhaps the greatest musical light of the entire Wesley family.

Of the Wesley clan J. A. Fuller Maitland, whose judgment carries weight, says:

Here we have an instance of family genius scarcely less remarkable than the Bachs in Germany. The race of the Wesleys was no less rich in musicians than in divines . . . Samuel and Samuel Sebastian Wesley must rank among the best English composers of their time.[11]

Speaking more specifically, Dannreuther, again writing for the *Oxford History of Music*, says:

The best examples of Samuel Sebastian Wesley contain an expression of the highest point up to that time reached by the combination of Hebrew and Christian sentiment in music. They are well worthy of comparison with Mendelssohn's *Psalms* and with the *Beatitudes* of Franck and of Liszt.[12]

Samuel Sebastian lived into a time when less antagonism against the Wesley name began to be felt among

[10] Lightwood, *op. cit.*, pp. 113-114.
[11] J. A. Fuller Maitland, *Music in the Nineteenth Century* (New York, 1902), p. 87.
[12] Dannreuther, *op. cit.*, p. 297.

the High Church party. Even he, however, with an acknowledged reputation as the greatest English Cathedral composer of his day, never attained the organ bench at St. Paul's or academic appointment to Oxford or Cambridge. Unfortunately, modern reprints of the works of Samuel and Samuel Sebastian Wesley give no idea of their true greatness, which ought to be known "wherever music is cherished and wherever the English language is spoken."[13] It is not a body of music which finds a ready audience today; the elder Wesley expressed himself most forcefully in his unaccompanied Latin motets (many of them still in manuscript at the British Museum) for which there is no ready place in either the Catholic or Protestant worship services of our day; and the principal works of Samuel Sebastian Wesley are Morning and Évening Services for the English Cathedral, which find no exact counterpart in the usage of this country.

In our own time, when the works of such men as Byrd and Tallis are still insufficiently known, small wonder should attach itself to the unperformed state of the works of the Wesleys, *père et fils*. But with the inevitable cycles of musical taste the day will come, perhaps soon, perhaps later, when these two men will cease being merely patronized by historians. In that better day their names will shine with the added luster that frequent performance inevitably and rightfully gives.

[13] *Ibid.*, p. 290.

XI. JOHN MASON NEALE
AND TRACTARIAN
HYMNODY

OTHER ENGLISH HYMN WRITERS OF the nineteenth century are undoubtedly greater favorites with the rank and file of churchgoers than is John Mason Neale. Certain individual hymns by other nineteenth-century writers—"Holy, Holy, Holy," "Nearer, My God, to Thee," "Just As I Am," and "Onward, Christian Soldiers," for instance—have vastly outstripped even the most popular of Neale's hymns in public favor. And yet, by virtue of the total number of his original and translated hymns included in present-day hymnals, John Mason Neale probably deserves to rank higher than any other nineteenth-century hymn writer in the public estimation.

Both the Methodist and Presbyterian hymnals include a greater number of hymns (originals and translations) by Neale than by any other nineteenth-century author. The 1940 Hymnal of the Protestant Episcopal Church lists a total of thirty-nine items derived from Neale; Charles Wesley, who ranks second to Neale, is represented by a total of eighteen—less than half as many. Among the top three or four "authors" in each of these three hymnbooks are Isaac Watts, Charles Wesley, and John Mason Neale. (Watts draws the highest score with the Presbyterians, Wesley with the Methodists, and Neale with the Episcopalians.) On a numerical basis, then, Neale contends with the more famous hymnists, Watts and Wesley, for top place in each of these three representative hymnals.

Though Neale has often been thought of as a mere translator of hymns, rather than an original author, many of his so-called "translations" owe little except a brief snatch here and there to their "originals"—and even the most literal "translations" frequently owe more of their success to Neale with his uncanny felicity in language than they do to the authors of the professed originals.[1] Certainly Neale deserves, at the very least, the same credit for "Jerusalem the Golden," "Brief Life is Here Our Portion," "All Glory, Laud and Honor," and "The Royal Banners Forward Go," to name at random a few of his translations, that Watts has received for "Our God, Our Help in Ages Past," or Joseph Addison for "The Spacious Firmament on High."

Besides the reputation of having been only a translator, other factors have prevented his achieving the recognition he deserves. For one thing, he never copyrighted any hymn he wrote, and spoke of casting his two mites into the Lord's treasury with no hope of reward.[2] Then again his hymns have been singularly slow in associating themselves with truly successful tunes. Because his ideal was Gregorian music, he disparaged tunes of the successful Victorian type. New-

[1] When criticized for publishing as "translations" some of his own original hymns, he admitted (*Hymns of the Eastern Church*, 1866): "The Hymns at pages 206, 209, and 'Art thou weary,' contain so little that is from the Greek, that they ought not to have been included in this collection."

[2] John Mason Neale, *Collected Hymns, Sequences, and Carols* (London, 1914), p. ii (quoted from Preface to *Joys and Glories of Paradise*, Jan. 10, 1865).

man once ascribed the tremendous popularity of "Lead, Kindly Light" to Dykes's tune, and he was right.[3] Neale's hymn, also set by Dykes, "Christian, Dost Thou See Them," has shown in his own case how helpful a good tune of the Victorian type may be in winning general acceptance for a hymn. We may therefore conclude that when really successful tunes are found for certain other of Neale's hymns his name will gain considerably in luster.

For various reasons (some of them not entirely commendable) Neale's life story, morever, has not been widely advertised, even among members of his own communion. Percy Dearmer a few years ago in *Songs of Praise Discussed* called Neale "the most learned hymnologist and liturgiologist of his time." Other Anglican writers of our own generation have followed Dr. Dearmer in praising Neale for his dual contribution as scholar and as hymn-writer. But while lauding him as a scholar and hymnist, Anglicans and their Episcopalian kinsmen have curiously refrained from publishing the full facts of his ecclesiastical career. What is there about it that should be concealed?

In the *Hymns Ancient and Modern* article (1909) assuredly the most crucial event in Neale's entire priestly career was blandly ignored—namely, the inhibition

[3] In the 1873 edition of *Apologia pro Vita Sua* Newman said of the words of "Lead, Kindly Light": "They are not a hymn, nor are they suitable for singing; and it is that which at once surprises and gratifies me, and makes me thankful, that, in spite of having no claim to be a hymn, they have made their way into so many collections." On another occasion Newman said of "Lead, Kindly Light"—"But, you see, it is not the hymn, but the tune, that has gained the popularity. . . . The tune is Dykes's, and Dr. Dykes was a great master."

from his priestly functions which was laid upon him by the Bishop of Chichester, Neale's ecclesiastical superior, in 1847, and not formally removed until November, 1863 (less than three years before Neale died at the early age of forty-eight). When telling the life story of a hymnist belonging to another denomination than their own, the editors of the historical edition readily told the whole story. After Neale, for instance, in their alphabetical section came Joachim Neander. Neander, the historical edition tells us,

displayed such a spirit of independence . . . as to his own belief and religious exercises, . . . that he was suspended until he signed a declaration by which he bound himself not to repeat any of the acts complained of.

But we are not told in the immediately preceding article on Neale that he too displayed such a spirit of independence "as to his belief and religious exercises" that he too was suspended from the exercise of ecclesiastical functions.

The story of Neale's inhibition runs as follows. Early during 1847 the Bishop of Chichester "felt it his duty to stop Mr. Neale from continuing to debase the minds of these poor people with his spiritual haberdashery."[4] Neale first heard of his inhibition when he received on May 8 the following note from the bishop:

REVEREND SIR, I feel it to be my duty to inhibit you, and I do hereby inhibit you from the exercise of clerical functions in my diocese.

I am, Reverend Sir, your well-wisher in Christ,

A. T. CICESTER.[5]

[4] Eleanor A. Towle, *John Mason Neale, D.D., A Memoir* (London, 1906), p. 160.
[5] *Ibid.*, p. 159.

After several attempts to show he was indeed loyal to the Church of England, Neale two years later (in 1849) finally begged for at least tacit allowance to officiate in the Holy Communion.[6] This appeal was followed by a petition to the Bishop from Neale's "people" in 1851, but the Bishop merely replied that "Mr. Neale must have perplexed their minds with new and strange shows and observances."[7]

During these years (and until his death) Neale was acting as warden of a charitable foundation for old people in the small town of East Grinstead; Sackville College, the name of the foundation, did not designate a college in our sense of the word and Neale was primarily a caretaker, not a chaplain. The previous wardens were not clergymen, and the position itself was an inadequate provision for a man with family. He was appointed by the patron, Lord De la Warr; and therefore not even the Bishop's inhibition could prevent him from continuing to live in Sackville College as its warden (with a salary of £27 a year).

All this information the editors of the historical edition of *Hymns Ancient and Modern* decided should best be forgotten. Neither did they think it wise, for instance, to reveal that when Neale went to his first parish assignment, before ever encountering the Bishop of Chichester, he had already met a rebuff from one of the greatest bishops of the day, Bishop Charles Sumner of Winchester.

In the autumn of 1841, anxious to enter upon parochial work (he was ordained deacon, June 6, 1841), he

[6] *Letters of John Mason Neale, D.D., Selected and Edited by His Daughter* (London, 1910), p. 117.
[7] Towle, *op. cit.*, p. 161.

"had made up his mind," as he at the time wrote, "to take the first suitable curacy that offered, without exercising any choice in the matter."[8] But when he was called to St. Nicholas, Guilford, Bishop Sumner refused to license him. Neale's designs "were frustrated by the unforeseen action of the Bishop of Winchester. Moreover with the stigma of rejection from one Bishop upon him, he found it difficult to obtain another curacy."[9] To complete the list then of ecclesiastics who either censured or inhibited Neale it would be necessary to mention three of the foremost bishops of his epoch, those of Winchester, Chichester, and London.[10]

These inhibitions (an inhibition is "the command of a bishop or ecclestiastical judge, that a clergyman shall cease from exercising ministerial duty") do not weigh lightly upon the conscience of some present-day historians, who would palliate the facts. And instead of telling us that Sumner (whose greatest achievement was the translation of Milton's long-neglected Arian treatise, *De Doctrina Christiana*)[11] attempted to put a quietus on Neale's career, and then telling the further difficulties of his church life, these reticent Anglican scholars leave the blunter Scotsmen, James Moffatt and Millar Patrick, editors of the *Handbook to the Church Hymnary*, the task of telling the bitter truth: "His own

[8] *Ibid.*, p. 55.   [9] *Ibid.*, p. 56.
[10] The Bishop of London withdrew his inhibition in December, 1852; but the inhibition of Neale's own diocesan lasted until November, 1863. The Bishop of London inhibited Neale because in one of the latter's published sermons he seemed to have endorsed the doctrine of transubstantiation. See *Neale's Letters*, p. 197.
[11] Discovered in the State Paper Office in 1823, *De Doctrina* (published in 1825) revealed Milton to have been an Arian at the time he wrote *Paradise Lost*.

Church had no honours for him; even his D.D. came from America."[12]

Neale was an accomplished versifier from his earliest student days, and in after life was a consistent winner of the Seatonian Prize for Poetry. His friend, Webb, to whom the bulk of his intimate correspondence was addressed, at first thought Neale turned to hymn writing simply because hymns provided an outlet for "your own fatal facility of versifying."[13]

Webb reflected the Tractarian prejudice against hymns when he wrote to Neale: "I expect I shall loathe your Methodistical hymnizing. . . . It is the oddest thing to me that you have never slipped off that Evangelical slough."[14]   Not until the Tractarians learned from a study of early office books that hymns in the Western Church were sanctioned as early as A.D. 385 and 386, and in the Eastern Church were used still earlier than that, did they show any enthusiasm for the singing of hymns. For a man of Neale's stamp, who, as his biographer said, had "in matters of religion, not much reverence for anything of later date than the twelfth century,"[15] antiquity of usage decided in favor of hymns. In 1840, almost a year before he was ordained deacon, Neale wrote, "You know my general dislike to hymns."[16] Two years later his first collection of hymns, *Hymns for Children,* appeared. His motive

---

[12] James Moffatt and Millar Patrick, *Handbook to the Church Hymnary* (Oxford, 1935), p. 442.

[13] *Letters,* p. 124.

[14] Neale's father was an Evangelical clergyman.

[15] Towle, *op. cit.,* p. 64.

[16] *Letters,* p. 22.

in publishing hymns from first to last (and he prepared thirteen collections for publication, of which the last, *Original Sequences, Hymns, and Other Ecclesiastical Verses*, did not appear until shortly after his death in 1866) was always his overmastering concern for purity of doctrine in the English Church.

In Neale's opinion "the depression of the Church of England in the first thirty years of the present century was, in great measure, brought to pass by the heresy of hymns."[17] And by heresy of hymns, when Neale made this statement in 1849, he did not mean heresy of hymn-singing, but rather the singing of hymns which contained heretical doctrine. Neale found heretical doctrine in the hymns of Watts, the Wesleys, William Cowper, John Newton, and other less well known hymn writers. In an article for the October, 1849, *Christian Remembrancer* Neale set down in minute detail his considered opinions concerning the merits of his predecessors in the writing of English hymns. This lengthy article is an important one, and of its preparation Neale said in a letter written during the summer just before the article appeared:

Now in my article, which is a long one, I have taken pains to set forth what I am sure—and what I have been sure of ever since I thought at all on the subject—are the kind of practical suggestions we want. I was six months writing the article, and six years at least thinking of it.[18]

The title of the article indicates the broad scope of its contents, "English Hymnology: Its History and Prospects."

[17] *Christian Remembrancer*, LXVI (Oct., 1849), 340.
[18] *Letters*, p. 125.

In this article Neale at the very outset dismisses the metrical versions of the psalms—or rather "perversions of the Psalms" as he prefers to call them[19]—because he thinks them patently unsuited to Catholic worship. After a thrust at the heresies contained within the Tate and Brady version, he then transfers his attention to hymns. Watts, he discovers, drips with

downright heresy, the most striking (though unintentional) profanity and irreverence. . . . And we own that nothing more surprises us in Dr. Johnson's writings than that he should voluntarily have recommended the works of Watts for insertion among the British poets.[20]

Of the hymns of John and Charles Wesley he wrote: "The offensive vulgarity of some of the Wesleyan . . . compositions almost exceeds anything of the kind in Watts." After examining the 560 hymns included in the Wesleyan Hymnbook of 1800, he said: "It may be doubted whether any of the original hymns included in this book could possibly, and by any change, be included in an English hymnology."[21] He added: "If two *must* be selected from the five hundred and sixty of the Wesleyan Hymn-Book, they would be 'Jesu, lover of my soul,' and 'Happy soul, thy days are ended.' " The Wesley 1780 hymnbook was filled, according to Neale, with cant expressions:

It was the boast of Wesley in the Preface from which we have before made an extract [the Preface to the 1780 Hymnbook]—"Here are no cant expressions, no words without meaning; those who impute this to us, know not

[19] *Christian Remembrancer*, LXVI (Oct., 1849), 304.
[20] *Ibid.*, p. 308.
[21] *Ibid.*, p. 316.

what they say." Yet we will venture to assert that no Hymn-book, except the Moravian, contains half so much.

"Whitefield's Hymn-book contains specimens of profane vulgarity." On the other hand, "Rock of Ages" is acceptable, and even merits praise, because the last stanza of Toplady's hymn "is not quite unworthy to recall to mind that wonderful apostrophe" contained in the seventh stanza of the *Dies Irae*.[22]

"Probably the worst collection of hymns ever put forth is the Olney Book," Neale informs us. "In some of Cowper's there may be beauty: but Newton's are the very essence of doggerel." (Newton wrote "Glorious Things of Thee Are Spoken" and "How Sweet the Name of Jesus Sounds.") Neale sums up the case against Newton: "We may very safely affirm that Newton is quite out of the question for church purposes; or, indeed, for any hymn-book whatever, and in whatever sect."

If Neale's zeal for doctrinal purity was not highly esteemed in the England of his own day, he did have one bit of recognition towards the end of his life which cheered him—his honorary D.D. from the University of Hartford (not Harvard as some reference manuals including *The Hymnal 1940 Companion* have erroneously asserted). His English contemporaries were inclined to sneer at a D.D. awarded *in absentia* by Trinity College at Hartford, Connecticut, but Neale took it, and used the initials D.D. after his name during the last six years of his life. In a letter to Webb, Neale explained why he had accepted a degree which was the

[22] *Ibid.,* p. 319.

butt of English jokes. Neale wrote in December, a year after the award of the degree, the following explanation of his acceptance:

You do not know—as how should you?—how much better known I am in America than in England;—how much more liked;—how much more an authority . . . . Well: it would be mean in me—because some few fellows in London may laugh—to hurt the feelings of those in America who gave me all they had to give—(and the less, mind you, the more mean and unkind it would be). Go to the bottom of the matter—and how absurd is a D.D.—paid for—of one of our Universities![23]

Neale had felt constrained to apologize for accepting the degree from the very moment when the award of it was first mentioned. As early as 1855 (Neale was then thirty-seven), he wrote in a letter: "One thing more will amuse you; the University of Hartford, the organ, you know, of the American Church, has offered me a D.D."[24]

Without conspicuous tact after receiving from one of its institutions a D.D., he, however, wrote of the Episcopal hymnal adopted in General Convention: "A judgment of extreme charity only can hinder us from branding some of the compositions of the latter [the hymn-book] as undoubtedly heretical."[25] Because of his preoccupation with heresies, he refined his own translations, and even his original hymns, with such zeal for doctrinal

[23] Towle, *op. cit.*, p. 281.
[24] *Ibid.*, p. 279.
[25] *Christian Remembrancer*, LXVI (Oct., 1849), 335. The American Church has followed a consistent plan of approving its hymnal, but the Church of England has never committed itself to an official hymnal for the whole Church.

"purity" that Roman Catholic theologians such as Father Aquinas Byrnes, a Dominican, have felt free to approve them: Neale (Byrnes said) is "ranked by most critics as the most eminent and brilliant translator of Latin and Greek hymns."[26] Thirty-one translations by Neale were published (1924) in *The Hymns of the Breviary and Missal* with an imprimatur by Patrick Cardinal Hayes."[27] He is, moreover, the only non-Roman Catholic translator whom modern Roman Catholic editors extol. He even pioneered in showing Roman Catholics the superiority of their medieval hymns over the officious "corrections" of those hymns undertaken by the last Humanist Pope, Urban VIII.[28] And if Neale did not know that Charles Wesley wrote "Hark, the Herald Angels Sing," albeit with a slight first-line change by Whitefield, at least he did know more about Venantius Fortunatus and Bernard of Morlaix than any one of his generation.

Neale's place is therefore secure; the editors of both Catholic and Protestant hymnbooks have insured his stock with future generations. All that these editors of hymnbooks and hymnal companions[29] need now do, if they really wish to assist us in our understanding of Neale, is to reveal the whole story of his life.

[26] Aquinas Byrnes, *The Hymns of the Dominican Missal and Breviary* (St. Louis, 1943), p. 678. Of the 189 hymns in this collection 51 are translations by Neale; 59 by Byrnes.

[27] Matthew Britt, *The Hymns of the Breviary and Missal* (New York, 1924); imprimatur dated 1922.

[28] J. Vincent Higginson, in the *Catholic Choirmaster* (March, 1948), p. 12. "He [John Mason Neale] proposed the use of the Sarum version which was unmarred by the classicists of the time of Urban VIII who often sacrificed many beauties 'to cramp the grand old hymns into the rules of prosody.'"

[29] *The Hymnal 1940 Companion* (New York, 1949), p. 512.

XII. IRA D. SANKEY AND THE GROWTH OF "GOSPEL HYMNODY"

B Y WHAT CRITERIA SHALL THE greatness of a musical composer be measured? By the numbers of copies his music has sold? By the amount of recognition he received from important personages during his own lifetime? By the stir his comings and goings made in newspapers? And by what standards, more especially, shall we measure the greatness of a composer in the sacred field? Shall his worth be measured in such terms as these: numbers of persons who have been added to church membership rolls or have responded to altar calls or have visited inquiry rooms under the influence of his music?

If any of these criteria are accepted as determinative of true greatness, then Ira D. Sankey, unrecognized as he is by historians of serious music, deserves an important niche in the musical pantheon; and if we accept lengthy convert lists as a measure of efficacy in sacred music, then Sankey, composer of "The Ninety and Nine" and of "I Am Praying For You," vastly exceeds in importance such another well-known figure in sacred music history as J. S. Bach. *Salvation Songs and Solos* has undoubtedly "saved" millions. Whether any composition by Bach, on the other hand, has ever brought even a single person to the altar for a confession of sin or into the inquiry room for pastoral prayer is doubtful.

Only one of Bach's two hundred cantatas was published during his lifetime. On the other hand, everything that Ira D. Sankey wrote was immediately published and avidly bought; one collection of his sold in England alone eighty million copies within fifty years after its initial publication.[1] During a brief four months in London on his 1875 tour, Sankey sang such songs of his as "I Am Praying For You," "Yet There Is Room," "It Passeth Knowledge," "The Ninety and Nine," and others of the same type, to an astronomical audience of over two million five hundred thousand people.[2] It is an open question, on the other hand, whether 2,-500,000 persons as an aggregate total listened to actual performances of such masterworks of Bach as his passions or his masses during the entire nineteenth century.

During that one memorable year, 1875, when all Britain seemingly flocked to hear Sankey's songs as he rendered them in the Moody services, even Queen Victoria thought of hearing Sankey, although she decided against attending the meetings an account of the enormous press of the crowds. She wrote in a letter, "It would never do for *me* to go to a public place to hear them, . . . nor, as you know, do I go to *any large public places now.*"[3] William Gladstone, Prime Minister, did, however, hear Sankey's renditions of his songs, and a man like Lord Shaftesbury could assert that had Moody and Sankey "done nothing more than teach the people to sing such hymns as 'Hold the Fort, For I Am

[1] *The Ira D. Sankey Centenary* (New Castle, Pennsylvania, 1941), p. 35.
[2] W. R. Moody, *The Life of Dwight L. Moody* (New York, 1900), p. 251.
[3] W. R. Moody, *D. L. Moody* (New York, 1930), p. 213.

Coming', they would have conferred an inestimable
blessing on Great Britain."[4]

The largest crowd ever assembled in New York history heard Sankey's songs at the New York Hippodrome during the 1876 Christian Convention. William
Lyon Phelps, testifying to the power of Sankey's music
not in New York but in Hartford during a later tour,
spoke of it as "enormously affecting." Phelps remembered that Sankey "played his own accompaniment.
... He had a way of pausing between lines of the song,
and in that pause the vast audience remained absolutely
silent."[5] A sophisticated music critic wrote of the overwhelming power that emanated from Sankey's renditions: "Even the critical musician will allow its prodi-
gious grandeur—a grandeur far different from that of
a Handel festival, but more impressive, as it is natural,
spontaneous, and enthusiastic."[6] That it was not alone
Sankey's powers as a singer, but also his powers as a
composer that drew such extravagant devotion, is perhaps obvious when we read another trained musical ob-
server's remarks:

A very erroneous opinion seems to exist among some people
that this gentleman is an accomplished singer. Nothing can
be further from the truth. Mr. Sankey has no pretensions
of the kind and we question if he could vocalize properly
the simplest exercise in the instruction book. He has possibly
never had a singing lesson in his life. His voice is a powerful baritone of small compass.

[4] *The Ira D. Stankey Centenary*, pp. 88-89. P. P. Bliss wrote
"Hold the Fort."
[5] *Ibid.*, p. 97.
[6] Gamaliel Bradford, *D. L. Moody* (New York, 1927), p. 183.

And yet it was this singer with "no pretensions of any kind" who because he sang "with the conviction that souls were receiving Jesus between one note and the next"[7] was able to tour England, Scotland, the United States, everywhere triumphing; in the heyday of his touring he went as far afield as Egypt, Palestine, and appeared even in manifestly unfriendly environments reaping adulation and applause such as only the most successful opera stars have gained.

Who was this Sankey? His life story began unmusically. His father, like the father of Stephen Foster, enjoyed local prominence in Western Pennsylvania politics. During a period of time when William Foster was serving as mayor of Allegheny, Pennsylvania, David Sankey, father of Ira Sankey, was serving a term in the Pennsylvania legislature, representing Lawrence County. The only approach to music study he seems to have made occurred in 1860 when he took a short trip to Farmington, Ohio, where he met William Bradbury, composer of the music for "He Leadeth Me," "Just As I Am," and other favorites; Bradbury was a trained organist and choirmaster with years of European study and travel in his background. Just how much Sankey could have gathered from him in a brief singing convention is, however, not ascertainable. During the Civil War Sankey (unlike Moody, whose coadjutor he was later to become) actually served in the Union Army, completing his service as a sergeant. He took a minor position in government service, and married the daughter of a state senator. He was elected

[7] *Ibid.*, p. 170.

Secretary of the Young Men's Christian Association in New Castle in 1867, and went to Indianapolis as a delegate to a YMCA convention in 1870. There he met D. L. Moody.

Moody, already one of the great names in American evangelism, immediately perceived Sankey's potential usefulness upon hearing Sankey rouse a slumbering audience into enthusiastic singing. "I have been looking for you for eight years," Moody told Sankey. Moody was an unmusical man himself; his early days in Sunday School work had, however, convinced him of the immense usefulness of music in religious meetings. He used singing in his Chicago Sunday School in order to attract the gamins in off the streets, and to keep them happy after they got inside his barn. Whenever discipline lagged, music was interjected; once, for instance, he decided to thrash a recalcitrant pupil, but before grabbing the young man and hustling him off into the cloakroom he directed the Sunday School to start singing as loudly as possible a familiar hymn. On another occasion a woman overpowered with excitement grew hysterical, whereupon Moody immediately called for the singing of "Rock of Ages" while the ushers carried the lady out. Moody could not himself distinguish one tune from another, as his son later testified,[8] and his approach to music was entirely pragmatic. In music as such he manifested no interest, but in music as a tool he was immensely interested. Any tool that he could use in evangelism was avidly scrutinized and then used in his own individual way.

[8] W. R. Moody, *D. L. Moody*, p. 198.

Moody called Sankey with the urgency of the New Testament imperatives: "Follow me!" Sankey followed Moody to England in 1873 at a guaranteed salary of one hundred dollars a month. Beginning very modestly in York with a small meeting in which only eight were present, the pair mushroomed into the most famous religious figures of the epoch. In Scotland Sankey achieved a major victory. Faced by the Calvinist prejudices against solo singing and against organ accompaniments, he overcame both objections. He tactfully used (as text for the first of his original songs composed for the Scottish meetings) verses by Dr. Horatius Bonar, pastor of the Chalmers Memorial Free Church, Edinburgh. "Yet There Is Room," their first joint venture, won immediate acclaim. Sankey before sitting down to play his own accompaniments at his small reed Estey organ always prayed with the congregation that God would bless his singing and use the music to bring salvation to many hungry, lost souls. This intimate approach prefaced by prayer helped to dispel the antagonism of the "unco guid" who hated organs as they hated sin. On only one occasion is it recorded that a startled worshiper unprepared for the sight of an organ in church rose rigidly, and rushed from the hall, crying, "Let me oot, let me oot. What would John Knox say of the both of ye?" The opinion of the many was expressed by a prominent professor from Free Church College, Edinburgh, who said:

It is amusing to observe how entirely the latent distrust of Mr. Sankey's "kist o'whistles" [organ] has disappeared. There are different ways of using the organ. There are organs in some churches for mere display, as someone has

said, "with a devil in every pipe," but a small harmonium designed to keep a tune right is a different matter, and is seen
to be no hindrance to the devout and spiritual worship of
God.[9]

What Calvin's reaction would have been to this refined example of reasoning is haplessly unobtainable.
Sankey achieved a victory over Scottish conscience that
the music of Bach or Handel or any other superlative
organist had never been able to achieve. An American
Methodist invading the stronghold of Knox achieved
the hitherto impossible. Publicizing the most spectacu-
lar series of meetings in Scottish history, Moody immediately "suggested that a fund of two thousand
pounds be raised to send reports of the meetings . . . to
all ministers in the United Kingdom."[10]

Sankey's methods were spectacularly successful; even
such penetrating observers as Matthew Arnold, certainly no friend of American emotionalism, recognized
the validity of the Sankey approach. Matthew Arnold
in *God and the Bible* took to task the uninformed
scientist who presumes to trifle with the great truths
of religion, criticizing specifically one unenlightened
scientist who grossly misunderstood the flux and flow of
Christianity through the centuries. Compared with a
scientist who knows nothing of the processes of history,
Matthew Arnold declared that "Moody and Sankey
are masters of the philosophy of history." Arnold
felt the influence of uninformed "professors" who know
nothing of the process of time to be pernicious; such

[9] W. R. Moody, *The Life of Dwight L. Moody*, p. 186.
[10] W. R. Moody, *D. L. Moody*, p. 159.

persons "instead of listening to the solemn and rhythmical beat" of the waves that come and go in man's spiritual history, choose instead "to fill the air with their own whoopings to start the echo. But the mass of plain people hear such talk with impatient indignation, and flock all the more eagerly to hear Messrs. Moody and Sankey."[11] Arnold continued:

They [the mass of plain people] feel that the brilliant free-thinker and revolutionist talks about their religion and yet is all abroad in it, does not know either that or the great facts of human life; and they go to the people who know them better. And the plain people are not wrong. Compared with Professor Clifford, Messrs. Moody and Sankey are masters of the philosophy of history.

Although Sankey was an innovator in Scotland when he finally persuaded congregations there to sanction an organ, and though he was the first, as George Stebbins tells us, to coin the name "Gospel Hymns" for folk-like tunes with enormous popular appeal, his theology was entirely conservative. In 1899, the year of Moody's death, long after Moody had dismissed Sankey from his service because of Sankey's failing health (although Sankey, of course, outlived Moody), Sankey wrote this short summary of his faith: "Hold fast to the good old ways of our fathers;—believing the good old Bible from back to back . . . I have found no new way to heaven."[12]

Sankey's influence today remains vital; a recent British hymnal, *Hymns of Prayer and Praise,* published by

[11] Matthew Arnold, *God and the Bible* (London, 1904), p. xvi.
[12] *Ira D. Sankey Centenary,* p. 68.

the Oxford University Press, includes seventeen Sankey hymns. The 1938 hymnal of the Church of England in Canada includes three.[13]   Although Sankey was a Methodist, the Methodist hymnals have not given him any more attention than have the hymnals of other denominations and countries. Sankey was important because he was typical. Other gospel hymn writers were as prolific, and perhaps more inspired. George Coles Stebbins and Philip P. Bliss, to name only two other widely known composers of gospel melodies, contributed some of the best liked tunes of the gospel movement. Bliss, Sankey's senior by two years, died in a train wreck at Ashtabula in 1876. Bliss's "Pull for the Shore, Sailor," was a great favorite with Crown Prince Humbert of Italy, who learned it as a child from his Waldensian nurses. The Rector of St. Paul's Within-the-Walls, American Episcopal Church in Rome, used often to have "Pull For the Shore, Sailor," played on the carillon of his church in order to satisfy the royal appetite for this number.[14]

Gospel melodies of the Sankey-Bliss-Stebbins-Doane type have been the staple of evangelical hymnals published for use in mission areas. Even in his own lifetime people in as distant countries as Egypt knew the Sankey-type melodies, and called for them when he toured the Near East. Hymnals published during the past half century in China, Japan, Mexico, and South America, designed for evangelical situations (unfortunately or fortunately, depending on one's point of view),

[13] W. R. Runyan, "A Century of Sankey," *Moody Monthly* (1940), p. 655.
[14] Walter Lowrie, "St. Paul's Within-the-Walls," *Historical Magazine of the Protestant Episcopal Church* (March, 1950), p. 27.

have specialized in "gospel hymns." Sankey's best-selling autobiography, *My Life and the Story of Gospel Hymns,* contains hundreds of anecdotes testifying to the "power" of gospel hymnody.

Musicians have felt that "gospel hymnody" is not an unmitigated blessing. Moody and his "legions of light" have generally treated music as a utilitarian art—not a fine art. As long as a piece of music demonstrates power to furrow fallow ground and prepare a crop of converts, music is welcomed. But the claims of music as an art with standards of excellence which are independent of the numbers of converts supplied—such claims are not always gladly recognized by those who think of music strictly in utilitarian terms.

At a mammoth celebration in his home town honoring the returned conquering hero, Sankey presented several large gifts to the citizens of New Castle. The notice of the Sankey celebration read in part:

The congregation then sang "There Is a Fountain Filled With Blood." The New Castle Octette next delighted the audience by giving "Rock of Ages," and they were followed by Rev. C. H. Dunlap, of the First Presbyterian Church, who offered a short prayer.[15]

D. L. Moody demanded short prayers, and he demanded music that would delight the audience. Gospel hymnody does delight audiences. In an epoch when the churches must enlist the support of thousands of people who know nothing about music as an art, but only as a species of entertainment, gospel hymnody is a necessity. When a long-winded preacher prayed too

[15] *Sankey Centenary,* p. 80.

lengthily, Moody, "who never loved long prayers and never made them, got impatient: 'While Brother Jones is finishing his prayer, let us all join in singing,'" Moody interrupted. Moody, who would interrupt even a prayer itself if he felt that the preacher was losing his audience, treated music, of course, with even more cavalier abandon. "He would have nothing whatever to do with a piece of music which only appealed to the sense of beauty." Moody's philosophy of music is a key to the understanding of the whole course of gospel hymnody. He judged music entirely in terms of its mass effect.

He could form no judgment . . . by hearing it played or sung in private. He must see it tried in a crowd, and could discover in an instant its adaptation to awaken the feelings which he needed to have in action. If it had the right ring he used it for all it was worth. "Let the people sing," he would shout—"let *all* the people sing. Sing that verse again. There's an old man over there who is not singing at all, let *him* sing." No matter how long it took, he would keep the people at work until they were fused and melted.[16]

This insensitivity to beauty in any of its forms—except as it appears in ethical conduct, the beauty of holiness—has caused many professional musicians to eschew gospel hymns. According to Kant's categorical imperative, every person deserves to be used not as a means towards some other objective, but as an end in himself. Professional musicians, quite naturally, have winced when they have been treated as means rather than as ends. Those musically minded persons who have been

[16] Bradford, *op. cit.*, p. 168.

ready to sacrifice all canons of artistic excellence in order to reach the largest number of persons have been happiest in their association with gospel hymnody.

Gospel hymnody has the distinction of being America's most typical contribution to Christian song. Gospel hymnody has been a plough digging up the hardened surfaces of pavemented minds. Its very obviousness has been its strength. Where delicacy or dignity can make no impress, gospel hymnody stands up triumphing. In an age when religion must win mass approval in order to survive, in an age when religion must at least win a majority vote from the electorate, gospel hymnody is inevitable. Sankey's songs are true folk music of the people. Dan Emmett and Stephen Foster only did in secular music what Ira D. Sankey and P. P. Bliss did as validly and effectively in sacred music.

APPENDICES

I. TWENTIETH-CENTURY PAPAL PRONOUNCEMENTS ON MUSIC

THE IMPACT OF PAPAL TEACHING IN THE UNITED STATES

ONE OF POPE PIUS X'S FIRST OFFIcial acts after his accession to the papacy in 1903 was the issuing of an encyclical letter on church music, *Motu Proprio*. His successor, Benedict XV, in a letter written on the occasion of the 1921 Palestrina celebration, called for renewed emphasis upon the principles of church music laid down in the *Motu Proprio* of 1903. Pius XI, who followed Benedict XV, issued a letter in December, 1928 (timing it to coincide with the twenty-fifth anniversary of the *Motu Proprio*), in which he asked for zealous devotion to the principles enunciated in Pius X's 1903 encyclical. An important recent papal encyclical dealing with church music, the *Mediator Dei* of Pius XII, was issued in November of 1947. Each of these four popes of the twentieth century, then, has had something to say on the subject of church music.

Pius X himself designated the *Motu Proprio* as a "juridical code of music" to which he wished "the force of law to be given."[1] Since within it is contained the fullest and most explicit formulation of a papal theory of music in modern times, and since Pius X is-

[1] For text of the *Motu Proprio* in an officially approved translation, see Sir Richard Runciman Terry's *The Music of the Roman Rite* (London, 1931), pp. 253-269.

sued it not as a private expression of his own personal
opinion but rather as a code to which he willed "with
the fulness of Our Apostolic Authority that the force of
law be given," this 1903 encyclical is a basic document
which must be studied by all who seek to understand
the present status of music in the Roman Catholic
Church.

Church music has seriously deteriorated during recent times, Pius X felt; in his opinion it suffered at
the beginning of the twentieth century from a "general
tendency to deviate from the right rule."[2]   After laying
it down as the "right rule" that "nothing which may
give reasonable cause for disgust or scandal" should be
allowed to intrude itself into public worship, he then
went on in the *Motu Proprio* to observe that of the various abuses causing disgust and scandal none was more
prevalent than "the abuse affecting sacred chant and
music."[3]

Furthermore he seems to have felt that the constant
intrusion of cheap and meretricious music into the most
solemn and important worship functions of the Catholic
Church could not be stopped by any mere gesture, any
mere polite wave of the hand.   He seems to have
recognized that in order to effect any widespread and
lasting improvement a juridical code possessing the
force of law and sanctioned by "Our Apostolic Authority" was required.

He asked for the elimination of all cheap, tawdry,
and profane music, and especially for the elimination
of all music composed in operatic style.   He called for

[2] *Ibid.*, p. 254.
[3] *Ibid.*, p. 253.

a return to Gregorian chant. He pointed out that not only has Gregorian chant always been regarded as the peculiar heritage of the Catholic Church, and therefore a type of music that is her very own, but also that "Gregorian chant has always been regarded as the supreme model for sacred music."[4] Pope Pius X was, of course, saying nothing very novel when he pointed out the virtues of Gregorian chant. But from long practical experience as a priest at Treviso, as a bishop at Mantua, and as an archbishop at Venice, he seems to have decided that (during his own generation, at least) lip service was oftener being given the Gregorian chant than any really hearty and intelligent use.

Musical abuse, as he had seen from his experiences at Treviso, Mantua, and Venice, is " one of the most difficult to eradicate,"[5] because "many prejudices on the matter" exist; and these prejudices, though frequently "lightly introduced," are often "so tenaciously maintained even among responsible and pious persons"[6] that the removal of this running sore is not infrequently opposed by the very authorities who should sponsor the surgery. Feeling, however, that surgery could no longer be safely postponed, he asked that the knife be first used to excise all music with distinctively secular associations.

He then suggested ways of binding up the wounds which would necessarily result from such deep cutting into the diseased tissues of church music. He asked bishops everywhere, for instance, to institute in their

[4] *Ibid.*, p. 256.
[5] *Ibid.*, p. 253.
[6] *Ibid.*, p. 254.

dioceses special commissions composed of persons "really competent in sacred music," and to entrust to these commissions "the task of watching over the music executed in their churches."[7] He then added this suggestion: "Nor are they to see merely that the music is good in itself, but also that it is adapted to the powers of the singers and is always well executed." He asked, moreover, for "diligence and love" in the promotion of sacred music studies at ecclesiastical seminaries.[8] He asked for the foundation of schools of liturgical music in order that professional musicians might secure their training under church auspices. He asked also for the restoration of the ancient *Scholae Cantorum*—choir schools attached to churches—and for the foundation of new *Scholae Cantorum*.

This encyclical letter, had it been taken everywhere as seriously as Pope Pius X evidently intended it should have been taken, would undoubtedly have inspired major improvements. In some few places it was, as a matter of fact, taken seriously. In the United States, to cite an example, a school of liturgical music was founded at the Manhattanville College of the Sacred Heart; this Pius X School of Liturgical Music has provided invaluable training in correct principles of chant and of polyphonic singing. But in the United States as a whole there has not been evinced any astounding interest in Pius X's *Motu Proprio*. What Ralph Adams Cram said of Catholic art: "Catholic art, particularly in

---

[7] *Ibid.*, p. 262.

[8] "Let the superiors be liberal of praise and encouragement," Pius X asks. He himself had while a seminary instructor set an example of leadership in training the seminarians to sing Gregorian chant.

the United States and Canada, reached the lowest point achieved by any art, religious or secular, within the historic period,"[9] is a statement that probably applies with considerable propriety to Catholic music as well as Catholic art in America.

When Pius X spoke it may have been his intention to speak with the authority of Moses when he said to Pharaoh, Let my people go from this Egyptian bondage. But the bondage to execrable music, no matter how great the authority of Moses, has not been so easily ended. Catholic writers conversant with music have repeatedly listed in such magazines as *Caecilia* and the *Catholic Choirmaster* the noxious plagues that have befallen Catholic congregations in this country. But in the United States, despite the constant suffering caused by the plagues of bad singing, bad organ playing, and bad choice of compositions, Pharaoh's heart thus far seems to have been hardened. The Pope's words have not been heeded, and only a miraculous deliverance at the Red Sea seems likely to end the bondage.

Other aspects of Pius X's teaching have not gone unheeded; certainly his strictures against Modernism have been heard. But since music has not always been considered to lie within the scope of faith and morals, papal pronouncements on music have not made a deep impress even when the music of the sanctuary has been discussed. Pius X's teachings on church music have certainly not been shoved aside simply because other

[9] See Theodore Maynard, *The Story of American Catholicism* (New York, 1942), p. 571. Maynard, after surveying the cultural scene, quotes George Shuster, president of Hunter College: "A terrible contempt for thought and loveliness has settled upon American Catholicism" (p. 585).

succeeding popes have failed to endorse his musical
philosophy.

Benedict XV wrote to the Dean of the Sacred
College on September 19, 1921:

We are unwilling that the passage of time should weaken the
force of those wise rules laid down by that Pontiff in his
Motu Proprio of 22nd November, 1903, and called by him
"The juridical Code of Sacred Music"; in fact We desire
them to obtain their full force especially as regards the classical polyphony.[10]

In the *Divini Cultus* of 1928 Pope Pius XI added his
own personal endorsement to the wise teachings of the
Motu Proprio on the subject of liturgical participation.
Pius XII in his encyclical, *Mediator Dei* (1947), quoted
with approval the following extract from Pius XI's
Divini Cultus: "So that the faithful take a more active
part in divine worship, let Gregorian chant be restored
to popular use in the parts proper to the people."[11]
Pius XII has added his endorsement to the endorsement already given by Pius XI: Gregorian music or
other music following the musical ideals embodied in
Gregorian chant should be used. The congregation as
well as the choir should learn how to sing chant.

But despite the earnest exhortations of Pius X, and
the added emphasis given them by Benedict XIV, Pius
XI, and Pius XII, this is what Monsignor Robert E.
Brennan, speaking before the annual meeting of the

[10] Terry, *op. cit.*, provides an English translation of Pope Benedict's letter to Vincent Cardinal Vannutelli on pp. 283-284.
[11] Pope Pius XII, *Mediator Dei*, ed. Gerald Ellard, S. J. (New
York, 1948), p. 75 (quoting Pius XI, *Divini Cultus*, 9).

National Catholic Education Association in 1948, had to say:

The *Motu Proprio* was issued forty-four years, almost to the day, before the *Mediator Dei;* and where is the diocese in our country that can boast of anything that approaches a custom, much less a tradition, of active participation by the faithful in the solemn Liturgy? . . . After forty-four years, the cause of sacred music remains largely a children's crusade, a project for individual pastors, and the excuse for the dubious activity of an occasional "Diocesan Director of Music."[12]

Writing in the August 10, 1946, issue of *America*, the national Jesuit weekly, Duncan Buchanan with a turn of Gaelic wit observed:

If only some of our non-Catholic friends would read the lucid and comprehensive directions given by His Holiness and then listen to the music in some of our churches and schools, they would be completely cured of their favorite notion that we are "pope-ridden."[13]

Among the specific abuses which Mr. Buchanan listed were (1) the wretched and callow hymn-tunes that are customarily favored, (2) the inappropriate and nauseous organ music often played during Mass, (3) the frequent ruthless trampling underfoot of decent standards in musical performance.

Father John LaFarge, well-known editor, remarked in another issue of *America* shortly after the appearance of Duncan Buchanan's article:

[12] National Catholic Educational Association, *Proceedings and Addresses, Forty-fifth Annual Meeting, 1948,* p. 123.
[13] Duncan Buchanan, "Cantate Domino," *America,* Aug. 10, 1946, p. 445.

Any little rural church in French Canada can put this country quite to shame, on either count: the joyful ease with which the congregation sings the plainchant common [the Kyrie, Gloria, Credo, Sanctus, and Agnus Dei]; the skill with which the little choir or *Schola* renders the intricacies of the Proper.[14]

He pleaded in the same article for unity with the mind of the popes, not only on such essential matters as dogma, but also on such "non-essential" matters as church music.

Catholic church musicians who have expressed themselves publicly have deplored the low estate of liturgical music in American churches. However, as Monsignor Brennan observed, church musicians "will always bear the stigma of being 'just musicians.'" It can hardly be expected, then, that Catholic musicians should wield sufficient power in church circles to bring about the desired improvements. Instruction in music and provision for organs and choirs entail expense which can be ill-afforded when other more pressing demands confront American churches. A demand for excellence in church music can hardly be expected while endless demands for new schools, new hospitals, and new church buildings confront the leaders of the Roman Catholic Church in this country.

Since not even musicians who are themselves Catholic can muster sufficient sentiment in favor of announced papal musical policies to bring about any marked im-

[14] John LaFarge (*America*, Sept. 21, 1946) asks for a return to the great hymns such as the *Te Deum*, and pleads for congregational participation in the singing of the great hymns; however, he fully recognizes the practical difficulties that inhibit the use of Gregorian chant on a wide scale.

provements, musical critics who are outside the church can hardly hope to influence practice within the church.

Speaking of church music in an article in the *Saturday Review of Literature* Professor Paul Henry Lang, distinguished editor and author, said:

Only the artistically unfit continue to compose ritual music, and a more miserable, tawdry, tinsel-strewn collection than recent church music is hard to imagine.

It is a most curious fact that in our vastly expanded musical life church music, once the greatest pillar of the art of music, has been relegated to the lowest regions. . . . Throughout the Middle Ages and the Renaissance a great composer was synonymous with a church composer.

When the great feast days are upon us and a Catholic church wants to outdo itself, the choirmaster usually turns to Gounod's "Saint Cecilia Mass," written in the honey-flavored style of "Roméo et Juliette," or he turns to the compositions of some local worthy.[15]

Lang's strictures were more or less evenly divided in the article from which we have quoted between abuses in Protestant and in Catholic environments. A similar desire to assess the church music situation with complete impartiality as far as religious ties are concerned is apparent in the following article by Paul Chandler Hume written for the Washington *Post* of October 3, 1948:

We have frequently discussed in this column the deplorable estate of music in Protestant churches. Today we comment on the even poorer state of affairs in Catholic Church music. Few congregations are ever given opportunity to sing plain (or Gregorian) chant; few choirs sing it, and too often the

[15] P. H. Lang, "Church Music—What's Left of It," *Saturday Review of Literature*, June 29, 1946, p. 30.

priests of the Church either fail to encourage it, or even oppose it.

Paralleling this sad fact is the pitifully small list of hymns repeated over and over in most parish churches, few of which are worthy of the time or effort required to sing their saccharine measures. And this in the church with the greatest musical heritage in Christendom.[16]

The music problem has been solved, if solution it can be called, in many churches simply by eliminating all music from the Low Mass. The Low Mass is, of course, quite generally preferred by the Catholic public; it cannot be denied that the spectacle of a thronged church with the vast multitude in absolute silence exerts a powerful effect upon the imagination. On the other hand, it is to be regretted that a musician must always prefer silence when music of the kind officially prescribed by the popes themselves might enhance the solemnity of the liturgy. Pius XII said in the *Mediator Dei:*

A congregation that is devoutly present at the sacrifice . . . cannot keep silent, for "song befits the lover," and, as the ancient saying has it, "he who sings well prays twice."[17]

In the *Mediator Dei* Pope Pius XII spoke not only on church music but also on church art. In both fields he called for a sympathetic understanding of modern achievement. "It cannot be said that modern music and singing should be entirely excluded from Catholic worship," he stated. In conformity with this policy of friendliness, such artists as Matisse, Rouault, and Dali, to name three widely disparate figures, have been moved

[16] This article was reprinted in *Caecilia: A Catholic Review of Musical Art*, March-April, 1949, pp. 89-90.

[17] Pius XII, *Mediator Dei*, p. 75.

to create for church use. In the musical field a recent *Mass* by Igor Stravinsky has received considerable attention; Stravinsky's *Mass* was premiered at La Scala Opera House in Milan, but also has been heard in church during an actual celebration of Mass.[18] This policy of welcoming the new as well as the old may, if adopted widely, produce significant improvements in Catholic church music. Father John Boyd, a Jesuit, recently wrote:

Liturgical art is the human reaction to the Christian Revelation. Being human, it should have the time-place element inherent in human nature.

Admittedly Gregorian music has attained high perfection as a vehicle of Catholic worship. But to freeze church music in the Gregorian neume or church architecture in the Gothic arch would be fatal.[19]

On the highest policy-making level, the level of papal pronouncement, the need for radical improvement has been recognized; how the highest decisions will be trans-

[18] An interesting discussion of Stravinsky's *Mass* may be found in the *Month*, April, 1949. Edmund Rubbra says (p. 252): "In the new Mass he seems to have borrowed the medieval costumes of Jacopo da Bologna or Matheus de Perusio." And yet he adds (p. 254): "I feel that the genesis of the work lies more in the apprehension of the fascinating problems of timbre and texture raised by the words and form of the Mass than in any deeply-felt desire to clothe them with music of an equal spirituality."

The problem of creating a modern setting that will satisfy liturgical need has more suitably been solved in such a work as Ralph Vaughan-Williams's mass for twelve voices. Other well-known composers who have written masses within recent years include Poulenc and Roy Harris.

[19] John D. Boyd, writing in *America*, Sept. 21, 1946, added the following significant comment: "Personally, I have still to find Gregorian melodies to express as aptly as vernacular hymns what the Western heart means in hailing Our Lady . . . and Gregorian anthems to equal the Christmas carols that have grown out of the soil of the simple peasant heart."

lated into action at the local level yet remains to be seen in America. There are some who would argue that the present state of music in American Catholic churches is quite acceptable; Mass, these persons would say, is a spiritual discipline, and a musician who dislikes the music needs to undergo penance for his snobbery. Pope Pius XII said in *Mediator Dei* that at Mass "it is necessary that the people add something else, namely, the offering of themselves as a victim."[20]

However it seems extremely unlikely that when urging the people to offer themselves as victim, Pope Pius XII had any such idea in mind as some now have in mind when they urge musically sensitive people to "offer themselves as victim" at masses where music is heard.

The church musician, as far as music is concerned, may prefer to think with the popes, rather than with certain representatives of his in this country. The American Church, as Leo XIII saw over a half century ago in his *Testem Benevolentiae*, is handicapped because of extreme distance from "denominational headquarters." Any move which brings present practice in American churches closer to the expressed mind and will of twentieth-century popes[21] as far as music is concerned, will inevitably be hailed by all musicians, regardless of creed, as a major victory for the cause in this country.

[20] *Mediator Dei*, p. 47 (paragraph 98).

[21] Papal theory rises above the practice of the papal choir. On the subject of performance standards at Rome, See P. Samuel Rubio, "Congreso Internacional de Música Sagrada," *La Ciudad de Dios* (El Escorial), May-August, 1950, p. 401: "Choirs nowhere, if they are constructed on the Roman model, are really satisfactorily constituted; the Roman choirs sing in colorless fashion, without feeling, without precision, and often out-of-tune."

II. THE JEWISH *UNION HYMNAL*

THE HYMNAL WHICH RECEIVES the most considerable usage in Reform temples is the *Union Hymnal*. Compiled and published under the auspices of the Central Conference of American Rabbis, the first edition of this hymnal appeared in 1897, the second in 1914, and the third in 1932. Because the *Union Hymnal* has been the one hymnal compiled and published under direct authority of the Central Conference of American Rabbis (which is the spiritual governing body of Reform Judaism) this hymnal has quite naturally enjoyed greater prestige than any other hymnal thus far issued for Jewish use in America.

However, despite this prestige, and despite the rather considerable usage that this hymnal receives, it has been subjected to vigorous criticism by a host of Jewish musical authorities. It has not been criticized for any of the reasons that most Protestant hymnals are criticized. The level of musical quality is high throughout. The book in its present edition shows extraordinary care in the preparation of both music and texts. In every mechanical detail the book is beyond criticism. But Jewish musicians resent it; they resent it, and have resented it from its first issue in 1897, because it is not specifically enough a Jewish effort.

Of the three main branches in American Judaism, Reform, Conservative, and Orthodox, only Reform temples would use a hymnal. If Orthodox musicians criticize the *Union Hymnal* their criticisms can be discounted because Orthodox Judaism would not countenance the use of a hymnal anyway. In Orthodox synagogues the singing is done by a male cantor; he sings in Hebrew. He also sings unaccompanied, since organs are not allowed in Orthodox synagogues. But if Orthodox musicians are prevented from accepting the *Union Hymnal* simply because Orthodox religious teaching opposes congregational hymn-singing in English with organ support, Reform musicians on the other hand are bound by no such religious scruples. Why, then, have Reform musicians—affected by no misgivings of conscience—proved, nevertheless, almost as unfriendly to the officially endorsed *Union Hymnal*[1] as have their Orthodox colleagues?

Fundamentally, all the objections have centered around the lack of a specific Jewishness in music as well as in text. Rabbi Isaac Moses of the Central Synagogue in New York City, himself a hymnbook editor, said on one occasion:

It is eminently proper that hymn-books intended for Jewish worship should be Jewish in character, and that the hymns of prayer should be the products of Jewish authors. . . . A collection of fine poems and melodies culled from the hymnals of the different [Christian] Churches has no place in the Synagogue. Has the Jewish genius produced nothing of value that we must needs go begging at the doors of every denomination?[2]

[1] In Judaism each congregation is an autonomous unit, and no hymnal can therefore become obligatory in the way that, for instance, *The Methodist Hymnal* is obligatory in the Methodist Church.

[2] A. Z. Idelsohn, *Jewish Music in its Historical Development* (New York, 1929), p. 330.

The first edition of the *Union Hymnal* was precisely "a collection of fine poems and melodies culled from the hymnals of the different Churches." Naturally enough, Jewish musicians, whether Reform or Orthodox, asked themselves: "Has the Jewish genius produced nothing of value that we must needs go begging?" Of the approximately 150 items in the first edition of the *Union Hymnal* only 16 were traced to any traditional Jewish source. The tunes for well over 100 items in the first edition were "adaptations of German, English, and French Christian composers."[3] The harmonizations of the hymn tunes, moreover, were all four-part arrangements of the sort one encounters everywhere in Protestant hymnals of the nineteenth and twentieth centuries.

An attempt to increase the Jewish content of the *Union Hymnal* was apparent in the 1914 second edition. Of the 226 items in the second edition, more than 140, however, still made use of tunes derived from non-Jewish sources. And among the 50-odd tunes by Jewish composers, only 2[4] showed a distinctive Jewish flavor. Of the 40 traditional tunes listed as such, Professor A. Z. Idelsohn has shown that only 16 actually derive from traditional sources. In his authoritative text,

[3] *Ibid.*, p. 324.

[4] Nos. 7 and 77. No. 77 *(Yigdal)* is the one Jewish hymn that has become widely known in Christian circles. The *Yigdal* appears in nearly all the standard Protestant hymnals with the title "The God of Abraham Praise." Thomas Olivers, Wesleyan minister, heard the *Yigdal* sung in a London synagogue and made a verse translation about 1770. Idelsohn criticized the arrangement of the *Yigdal* music in the second edition of the *Union Hymnal* because it resembled too closely the four-part arrangement sung in Protestant Churches.

Jewish Music, he has moreover contended that several of the melodies that actually deserve to be called traditional were so mutilated in the 1914 edition as to be valueless for any student bent on learning the original character of the music.

The third edition attempted to stress Jewish elements. But the list of authors still included such men as Isaac Watts, William Cowper, James Montgomery, Robert Grant, William Cullen Bryant, John Greenleaf Whittier, Christopher Wordsworth, James Russell Lowell, Samuel Longfellow, William Walsham How, and John Ellerton, all of whom made conspicuous contributions to Protestant hymnology. The hymns from such authors as Bishop Wordsworth and Bishop How have, of course, been carefully chosen, but the fact remains that a very large proportion of hymns even in this third edition were not written by Jewish authors. Tunes as well as texts in this third edition were often borrowed. Examples of borrowings include Bach's setting of a Georg Neumark chorale; Handel's tune now associated with Nahum Tate's Christmas hymn, "While Shepherds Watched Their Flocks by Night"; Haydn's tune now associated with "O Worship the King"; Felice de Giardini's tune *Trinity,* now associated with "Come, Thou Almighty King"; William Croft's tune *St. Anne,* now associated with "Our God, Our Help in Ages Past." Indebtednesses, both in texts and tunes, can thus be easily demonstrated from a study of the contents of the *Union Hymnal* even in this third edition.

On the other hand, there are demonstrably more Jewish features in the third edition than there were in

the second, just as there were more Jewish features in
the second edition than there were in the first. The third
edition printed 267 English hymns in the main section
(Part I); of these 267 approximately 50, or one-fifth
of the total, are hymns founded on traditional synagogal
chants. A significant innovation in the third edition was
the large number of entirely new hymns. Of the 182
new hymns nearly all were written (or adapted from
Jewish sources) by Jewish composers. Christian
sources, as far as the new hymns were concerned, were
deliberately avoided. In the fourth edition of the
Union Hymnal, which has been promised, a much
larger percentage of specifically Jewish texts and tunes
will undoubtedly be included, and it is extremely likely
that the neutral material from Christian sources will no
longer appear.

The distinctive musical features in the third edition
that can be called specifically Jewish may be listed
briefly: (1) hymns based on "cantillation modes" or
"a traditional Yom Kippur mode," or "traditional Rosh
Hashanah modes" are included;[5] (2) hymns using the
augumented second, either in the harmony or in the
principal melody, can be found (the *Ahavoh-Rabboh*
mode);[6] (3) more than a third of the hymns depart
from the major mode, and melodic lines that suggest
such modes as the *Adonoy-Moloch* mode occur;[7] (4)

[5] Nos. 56, 143, 163, 157, 158, 159.
[6] No. 48 shows the augmented second in the upper melody; nos.
169 and 173 show the augmented second in an inner voice movement. See also Part II, nos. 323, 327; and (melisma) no. 318.
[7] For definition of these modes, see Idelsohn, *op. cit.*, pp. 478-479.

harmonizations which depart widely from accepted classical harmony are frequently found.[8]

As a surer grasp of the elements which may be considered specifically Jewish is obtained, Jewish composers will in the future be better able, no doubt, to fulfil the ever-increasing demand for tunes and for harmonizations that sound a distinctively Jewish note. In the past, ignorance of the national style has caused even the foremost composers to write music that has no authentic Jewish traits. Salomone Rossi never departed from the Jewish faith, yet wrote polyphonic music in the sixteenth and early seventeenth century that as music showed no Jewish traits. Even his Hebrew liturgical musical written for the Mantua congregation sounds like the standard polyphony of the other Italian composers of his own epoch.[9] Similarly in the nineteenth century Jewish composers (or composers of Jewish extraction) such as Meyerbeer, Halévy, Mendelssohn, Offenbach, Anton Rubinstein, and Carl Goldmark all wrote in the generally accepted idiom of their epoch, just as Rossi had written in the generally accepted idiom of his epoch. More recent composers, such as Mahler, Schönberg, Copland, Gershwin, and Irving Berlin, even when gladly acknowledging their Jewish origin, have shown small interest in Jewish sacred music. Among the composers of the twentieth century who enjoy international reputation it would seem that only Ernest Bloch has attempted to write any considerable

---

[8] The hymns of Achron all show more harmonic daring than is customary in Protestant hymnals.

[9] Paul Nettl, "Some Early Jewish Musicians," *Musical Quarterly* (Jan., 1931), p. 42.

body of music that can be called specifically Jewish.[10]

But composers of the future may show a different spirit. The large number of new books and articles on Jewish music shows a burgeoning national spirit. Schools also are even now being founded to train students in Jewish music. Just as Pius X desired the foundation of schools of Catholic music, so Jewish religious leaders desire the foundation of schools of Jewish music. The reign of Gentile organists and singers in the choir loft will abruptly end when there are Jewish organists and singers available to take their places. Reform temples which have given Gentile musicians an opportunity to double in Christian and in Jewish houses of worship will no longer need to depend upon Gentile talent when a generation of musicians has emerged from the new schools of Jewish liturgical music.

As long ago as July, 1929, Leonid Sabaneëv wrote:

On the average the Jewish race is by nature more musical than any other, and the number of Jewish musicians is considerably greater than that of other nationalities. . . . The Jews have always been a nation of singers, have always found in song an outlet for their agitating griefs, their temptations, their wrath. And now when that nation has singled out from itself an intellectual class, it not only can *but must speak to the world in a musical language of its own.*[11]

Sabaneëv italicized the very words that have been accepted by Jewish musicians quite generally as an axio-

[10] Leonard Bernstein's "Jeremiah Symphony" has not been followed up by other works religiously oriented.
[11] Leonid Sabaneëv, "The Jewish National School in Music," *Musical Quarterly*, July, 1929, p. 468.

matic truth, especially since the foundation of Israel. When the Israel Symphony made its United States tour in 1951 a lack of Jewish content was noted in the programs by Virgil Thomson, music editor for the New York *Herald-Tribune*. But the Israel Symphony played on that tour not only for its immediate friends but also for the wider public who have no special ties with the new state. The small amount of Jewish music included on the Israel Symphony programs may have reflected simply a desire to gratify the musical tastes of those who have no real understanding of Jewish musical traditions. But in religious music there is obviously no reason for pampering Gentile tastes. The time may now not be far distant when the fervent desire that Israel *speak to the world in a musical language of its own* ceases to be merely a pious expression of hope, and becomes instead a presently fulfilled reality.

The trend of the *Union Hymnal* follows the trend in Jewish cultural life as a whole. A distinctive Jewish flavor in music as well as text has been the objective that has guided successive revision committees, and will undoubtedly continue to be the objective which guides revision committees of the future. The trend in hymnal revision strikingly parallels the trends in Reform Judaism. The earliest Reformists were latitudinarians such as David Friedländer of Berlin, who at the end of the eighteenth century was ready to accommodate Judaism to everything in Christianity except Jesus as Second Person in the Triune Godhead. The famous Hamburg Temple, founded in 1817, similarly showed in its ritual and in its communal life a spirit of accommodation. An organ was installed as a gift from the uncle of the poet Heine; the spirit of Heine, who was ready to abandon everything distinctively Jewish, was apparent in the order of worship. Singing was patterned on Lutheran chorale singing, and a Cantor was engaged only to lead the responses.[12] But as time proved all things, the Hamburg Temple veered back to a much more conservative position *vis à vis* things Jewish. And the history of the Reform movement as a whole shows the same tendency to begin, as did the 1897 *Union Hymnal,* with extreme revision, and then to work progressively backward through succeeding revisions to a more and more conservative position.

Synagogue leaders, whether of Reform, Conservative, or Orthodox persuasion, unite nowadays in desiring that Jewish composers stand with feet firmly planted in the authentic Hebrew past. All would agree the time for worshiping at alien musical shrines has long passed. But if a statement of policy is easy enough to make, the implementation is more difficult. A synagogal repertory cannot be built simply by commissioning Jewish composers of our own day to write music on traditional themes. One of the most renowned of Jewish composers, Arnold Schönberg, wishing to write music for the synagogue, in 1938 completed a *Kol Nidre* for recitor, chorus, and orchestra, weaving his own kind of variations on the traditional theme. But when actually presented it had to be given in a hotel rather than a synagogue.[13]

[12] "Originally it was planned not to employ a *chazzan* at all" (Idelsohn, *op. cit.,* p. 240).

[13] Walter H. Rubsamen, "Schoenberg in America," *Musical Quarterly,* Oct., 1951, p. 476.

In order to find any real use in the synagogue, music composed for its functions must merit classification not simply as Jewish music but more specifically as Jewish worship music. The problems of creating such a body of distinctively Jewish worship music are difficult, but if the highway to their solution has not yet been clearly marked for the wayfaring man, it is at least certain, however, that synagogal leaders with their vision of the new Israel will not rest content until the right road has been found.

BIBLIOGRAPHY

The following short-title bibliography includes only works actually cited in the text. It does not include standard encyclopedias and dictionaries, nor does it include hymnals in present use.

Amos, Flora R. *Early Theories of Translation*. New York, 1920.

Anton, Karl. *Luther und die Musik*. Zwickau, 1928.

Archbishops of Canterbury and York. Committee on the Place of Music in the Worship of the Church. *Music in the Church*. London, 1951.

Arnold, Matthew. *God and the Bible*. London, 1904.

Austin, John. *Devotions in the Ancient Way of Offices*, 4th ed. Paris, 1685 (1st ed., Paris, 1668).

Augustine. *Confessions*, ed. J. Gibb and W. Montgomery. Cambridge, 1927.

Bainton, R. H. *Here I Stand*. New York, 1950.

Beck, F. A. *Dr. M. Luthers Gedanken über die Musik*. Berlin, 1825.

Benson, Louis F. *The Best Church Hymns*. Philadelphia, 1898.

———. *The Early Editions of Dr. Watts's Hymns*. Philadelphia, 1902.

———. *The English Hymn*. Philadelphia, 1915.

Bett, Henry. *The Hymns of Methodism*, 3rd ed. London, 1945.

Blume, Friedrich. *Johann Sebastian Bach*. Kassel, 1951.

Bradford, Gamaliel. *D. L. Moody*. New York, 1927.

Bridges, Robert, and Wooldridge, H. E. *The Yattendon Hymnal*. London, 1920.

Britt, Matthew. *The Hymns of the Breviary and Missal*. New York, 1924.

Buchanan, Duncan. "Cantate Domino," *America,* August 10, 1946.

Bukofzer, Manfred. *Music in the Baroque Era.* New York, 1947.

Burney, Charles. *An Account of the Musical Performances in Westminster Abbey.* London, 1785.

———. *A General History of Music.* London, 1776-89.

Buszin, Walter E. "Luther on Music," *Musical Quarterly,* January, 1946.

Byrnes, Aquinas. *The Hymns of the Dominican Missal and Breviary.* St. Louis, 1943.

Calvin, John. *Commentary on the Book of Psalms.* Edinburgh, 1845-1849.

———. *Homiliae in librum primum Samuelis.* Geneva, 1604.

———. *Sermons upon the Booke of Job,* tr. Golding. London, 1574.

Campbell, Sidney S. *Music in the Church.* London, 1951.

Carson, Alexander. *Examination of the Principles of Biblical Interpretation.* New York, 1855.

Catholic Church. *National Catholic Education Association, Proceedings and Addresses, 45th Annual Meeting.* 1948.

Church of England. *The Prayer Book of King Edward the Sixth, 1549* (facsimile reprint, 1844).

Cotton, John. *Singing of Psalmes a Gospel-Ordinance.* London, 1647.

Coverdale, Miles. *Goostly Psalmes and Spirituall Songes.*

Covert, W. C., and Laufer, C. W. *Handbook to the Hymnal.* Philadelphia, 1946.

Dalyell, Sir John Graham. *Musical Memoirs of Scotland.* Edinburgh, 1849.

Dannreuther, Edward. *The Oxford History of Music,* Vol. VI. London, 1905.

David, Hans T., and Mendel, A. *The Bach Reader*. New York, 1945.

Davis, Arthur P. *Isaac Watts*. New York, 1943.

Davison, Archibald T. *Protestant Church Music in America*. Cambridge, Mass., 1933.

Dearmer, Percy. *Songs of Praise Discussed*. London, 1933.

Domestic State Papers of Henry VIII, Vol. XVIII, pt. 2. London, 1920.

Douen, Orentin. *Clément Marot et le Psautier Huguenot*. Paris, 1878-79.

Douglas, Winfred. *Church Music in History and Practice*. New York, 1937.

Dryden, John. *The Works of John Dryden* (Scott-Saintsbury edition), Vol. XIV. Edinburgh, 1889.

Einstein, Alfred. *A Short History of Music*. New York, 1947.

Etherington, Charles L. *The Organist and Choirmaster*. New York, 1952.

Fellowes, E. H. *English Cathedral Music*. London, 1941.

FitzGerald, Edward. *Letters*. London, 1894.

Fletcher, Donald R. "English Psalmody and Isaac Watts." University Microfilms, Ann Arbor, Mich., 1951.

Flower, Newman. *George Frideric Handel*. New York, 1948.

Foote, Henry W. *Three Centuries of American Hymnody*. Cambridge, Mass., 1940.

Gabriel, Paul. *Das deutsche evangelische Kirchenlied von Martin Luther bis zur Gegenwart*. Berlin, 1951.

Gairdner, James. *The English Church in the Sixteenth Century*. London, 1902.

Garside, Charles. "Calvin's Preface to the Psalter: A Re-Appraisal," *Musical Quarterly*, October, 1951.

Gerber, C. G. *Historie der Kirchen-Ceremonien in Sachsen.* Dresden and Leipzig, 1732.

Glover, C. H. *Dr. Burney's Continental Travels, 1770-1772.* London, 1927.

Green, Richard. *The Works of John and Charles Wesley, A Bibliography.* London, 1896.

Gray, Cecil. *The History of Music.* New York, 1931.

Grisar, H. *Luther.* London, 1918.

Gurlitt, Wilibald. *Johann Sebastian Bach.* Kassel, 1947.

Hall, Edward. *The Triumphant Reigne of Henry VIII.* London, 1904.

Harford, George, and Stevenson, Morley. *The Prayer Book Dictionary.* London, 1925.

Hatfield, James T. "John Wesley's Translation of German Hymns," *PMLA,* XI (1896).

Herbert, Thomas W. *John Wesley as Editor and Author.* Princeton, N. J., 1940.

Hickes, George. *Devotions in the Ancient Way of Offices.* London, 1717.

Historical Manuscripts Commission. *Earl of Egmont MSS, Diary.* 1920.

Idelsohn, A. Z. *Jewish Music in Its Historical Development.* New York, 1929.

The Ira D. Sankey Centenary. New Castle, Penn., 1941.

Johnson, Samuel. *Lives of the English Poets.* Oxford, 1905.

Kahnis, Ch. Fred. Aug. *Internal History of German Protestantism.* Edinburgh, 1856.

Kidd, B. J. *Documents Illustrative of the Continental Reformation.* Oxford, 1911.

Lang, P. H. "Church Music—What's Left of It," *Saturday Review of Literature,* June 29, 1946.

Lee, Humphrey. *John Wesley and Modern Religion.* Nashville, 1936.

Leger, J. A. *La Jeunesse de Wesley*. Paris, 1910.

Leichtentritt, Hugo. *Music, History, and Ideas*. Cambridge, Mass., 1940.

Lightwood, James T. *Samuel Wesley, Musician*. London, 1937.

Lindsay, T. M. *History of the Reformation*. New York, 1928.

Lock, Walter. *John Keble: A Biography*. London, 1893.

Lowrie, Walter. "St. Paul's Within-the-Walls," *Historical Magazine of the Protestant Episcopal Church*, March, 1950.

Luther, Martin. *Christliche Geseng, Lateinisch und Deudsch*. Wittenberg, 1542.

———. *Opera Latina*, Vol. VIII. Frankfurt, 1873.

———. *Werke*, Vols. LIII, LVI, LX, LXII. Erlangen, 1826-57.

Lyell, James P. R. *Mrs. Piozzi and Isaac Watts*. London, 1934.

McCutchan, R. G. *Our Hymnody: A Manual of the Methodist Hymnal*. New York, 1937.

McMillan, William. *The Worship of the Scottish Reformed Church, 1550-1638*. Edinburgh, 1931.

McMurtrie, Douglas C. "A Bibliography of South Carolina Imprints, 1731-1740," *South Carolina Historical and Genealogical Magazine*, XXXIV (July, 1933).

Maskell, William. *Monumenta Ritualia Ecclesiae Anglicanae*, 2nd ed. Oxford, 1882.

Massachusetts Historical Society Proceedings (2nd series), Vol. IX. Boston, 1895.

Mather, Cotton. *Magnalia Christi Americana*. London, 1702.

Maxwell, William D. *An Outline of Christian Worship.* Oxford, 1936.

———. *The Liturgical Portions of the Genevan Service Book.* Edinburgh, 1931.

Maynard, Theodore. *The Story of American Catholicism.* New York, 1942.

Merbecke, John. *A Booke of Notes and Commonplaces.* London, 1581.

———. *The Booke of Common Praier noted.* London, 1550.

Moffatt, James. *Handbook to the Church Hymnary.* London, 1927.

Moffatt, James, and Patrick, Millar. *Handbook to the Church Hymnary.* Oxford, 1935.

Moody, W. R. *D. L. Moody.* New York, 1930.

———. *The Life of Dwight L. Moody.* New York, 1900.

Mosheim, J. von. *Institutes of Ecclesiastical History.* London, 1863.

Myers, R. M. *Handel's Messiah.* New York, 1948.

Naumann, Emil. *History of Music.* London, 1886.

Neale, John Mason. *Collected Hymns, Sequences, and Carols.* London, 1914.

———. "English Hymnology: Its History and Prospects," *Christian Remembrancer*, October, 1849.

———. *Herbert Tresham: A Tale of the Great Rebellion.* London, 1843.

———. *Hymns of the Eastern Church.* London, 1866.

———. *Letters of John Mason Neale, D.D.* London, 1910.

Nef, Karl. *An Outline History of Music.* New York, 1935.

—Nettl, Paul. *Luther and Music.* Philadelphia, 1948.

————. "Some Early Jewish Musicians," *Musical Quarterly*, January, 1931.

Newman, John. *Verses on Various Occasions*. London, 1903.

Nova Acta Historico-Ecclesiastica (Sechster Band, XLI-XLVIII Theil). Weimar, 1766.

Ollard, S. L. *A Dictionary of English Church History*. London, 1919.

Patrick, Millar. *Four Centuries of Scottish Psalmody*. London, 1949.

Phillimore, J. S. *Some Remarks on Translations and Translators*. Oxford, 1919.

Phillips, C. S. *Hymnody Past and Present*. London, 1937.

Pius X. *Motu Proprio* (in Terry, *The Music of the Roman Rite*).

Pius XII. *Mediator Dei*, ed. Gerald Ellard, S. J. New York, 1948.

Praetorius, Michael. *Syntagma Musicum*, Vol. I. Wittenberg, 1615.

Presbyterian Church. *Constitution of the Presbyterian Church in the United States of America*. Philadelphia, 1944.

————. *Manual for Church Officers and Members*, 15th ed. Philadelphia, 1947.

Preuss, Hans. *Bachs Bibliothek*. Leipzig, 1928.

Procter, Francis, and Frere, W. A. *A New History of The Book of Common Prayer*. London, 1901.

Prunières, H. *A New History of Music*. New York, 1943.

Pulver, Jeffrey. *A Dictionary of Old English Music*. London, 1923.

Rabinovitch, Israel. *Of Jewish Music, Ancient and Modern*. Montreal, 1952.

Rattenbury, J. Ernest. *The Conversion of the Wesleys.* London, 1938.

Rimbault, Edward F. *John Merbecke's Book of Common Prayer as used in the Chapel Royal of Edward VI.* London, 1845.

Romaine, William. *The Whole Works.* London, 1787.

Rothmüller, Aron M. *Die Musik der Juden.* Zürich, 1951.

Rubbra, Edmund. "Stravinsky's Mass," *The Month,* April, 1949.

Rubio, Samuel. "Congreso Internacional de Música Sagrada," *La Ciudad de Dios,* El Escorial (Spain), May-August, 1950.

Rubsamen, Walter H. "Schoenberg in America," *Musical Quarterly,* October, 1951.

Sabaneëv, Leonid. "The Jewish National School in Music," *Musical Quarterly,* July, 1929.

Saleski, Gdal. *Famous Musicians of Jewish Origin.* New York, 1949.

Sankey, Ira D. *My Life and the Story of Gospel Hymns.* Philadelphia, 1907.

Scheibe, J. A. *Cristischer Musikus.* Leipzig, 1745.

Scheide, William H. *Johann Sebastian Bach as a Biblical Interpreter.* Princeton, N. J., 1952.

Scholes, Percy A. *The Puritans and Music.* London, 1934.

Schroeder, H. J. *Canons and Decrees of the Council of Trent.* London, 1941.

Schweitzer, Albert. *J. S. Bach.* London, 1923.

Sendrey, Alfred. *Bibliography of Jewish Music.* New York, 1951.

Spitta, Philipp. *Johann Sebastian Bach.* London, 1899.

Strype, John. *Ecclesiastical Memorials,* Vol. II. Oxford, 1822.

Stuart, Moses. *Ernesti's Elements of Interpretation.* Andover, Mass., 1822.

Taylor, Sedley. *The Indebtedness of Handel.* Cambridge, 1906.

Terry, C. S. *Bach: A Biography.* London, 1933.

———. *Joh. Seb. Bach: Cantata Texts.* London, 1926.

Terry, Sir Richard R. *A Forgotten Psalter and Other Essays.* London, 1929.

———. "Forgotten Composers," *Musical News,* LXVIII, No. 1718.

———. "John Merbecke," *Proceedings of the Musical Association, Forty-Fifth Session, 1918-19.* Leeds, 1920.

———. *The Music of the Roman Rite.* London, 1931.

Thomas, Isaiah. *A History of Printing in America,* 2nd. ed. Albany, 1874.

Titcomb, Everett. *A Choirmaster's Notebook.* Boston, 1950.

Towle, Eleanor A. *John Mason Neale, D.D., A Memoir.* London, 1906.

Tudor Church Music, Vol. X. London, 1929.

Watts, Isaac. *Discourses, Essays, and Tracts, on Various Subjects.* London, 1753.

———. *Horae Lyricae, Poems Chiefly of the Lyric Kind.* London, 1706.

———. *Hymns and Spiritual Songs . . . With an Essay towards the Improvement of Christian Psalmody.* London, 1707.

———. *Reliquiae Juveniles: Miscellaneous Thoughts in Prose and Verse.* Glasgow, 1786.

———. *The Psalms of David Imitated in the Language of the New Testament.* London, 1719.

———. *The Works of the Late Reverend and Learned Isaac Watts,* Vol. IV. London, 1753.

Wesley, John. *Collection of Psalms and Hymns.* Charleston, S. C., 1737.

————. *Collection of Tunes Set to Music as they are commonly sung at the Foundery*. London, 1742.

————. *The Journal of the Rev. John Wesley, A.M.*, ed. Nehemiah Curnock. London, 1909-16.

————. *The Letters of the Rev. John Wesley, A.M.*, ed. John Telford. London, 1931.

————. *The Works of the Rev. John Wesley, A.M.*, Vols. II and VII. New York, 1856.

Wesley, John and Charles. *The Poetical Works*, collected and arranged by G. Osborn, Vol. II. London, 1869.

Wesley, Samuel. *Poems on Several Occasions*, 2nd ed. Cambridge, 1748.

Wooldridge, *Oxford History of Music, c. 1400-1600*. London, 1932.

Wustmann, Rudolf. *Musikgeschichte Leipzigs*. Leipzig, 1909.

Young, Percy M. *Handel*. London, 1947.

————. *The Oratorios of Handel*. London, 1949.

INDEX

Aaron, 103n.

Aberdeen University, organ destroyed at during 17th century, 17

Abraham, 66

Achitophel, adviser to Absalom, 96

Achron, Joseph (1886-1943), 182n.

Achsa[h] (*Joshua*), 88

Act Abolishing Diversity in Opinions (1539), 30-31, 33n., 35

"Adam and Christ, Lords of the Old and New Creation" (Watts's Psalm VIII), 94

Adami, J. C. (*Apfel in silberner Schaal oder Betrachtung des Hohen Liedes Salomonis*, 1708), 74

Addison, Joseph (1672-1719), 121, 140

Adonoy-Moloch mode, 181

Agnus Dei, position of (1549 Prayerbook), 28

Ahavoh-Rabboh mode, 181

Aldersgate, Wesley's conversion experience at (May 24, 1738), 112-114, 116

Alexander, known as "Balas" (d. 146 B.C., usurper, king of Syria), 90

Alexander Balus (1748), 90

Alexander's Feast (1736), 82

Allegheny (Pennsylvania), 154

"All Glory, Laud, and Honor" (Theodulph of Orleans, 820), 140

"All We Like Sheep Have Gone Astray" (*Messiah*), 83

America, Jesuit weekly, 171, 172n., 175n.

"And He Shall Purify the Sons of Levi" (*Messiah*), 83

Andover Seminary, 73

Anglican hymnal, "the first," 116, 129

Anne, Queen (reigned 1702-1714), 81n., 117

Anticalvinismus oder Unterredung der Reformirten Religion (August Pfeiffer), 46

Anton, Karl (b. 1887), 10n.

Apologia pro Vita Sua, 141n.

Arianism
  Milton's, 144
  Watts's 109

Arndt, Johann (1555-1621; author of *Von wahren Christenthum*), 51n.

Arnold, Matthew (1822-1888)
  opinion of Moody and Sankey, 157-158
  opinions on Watts's hymns, 111n.

Arnstadt, Bach's career at (1703-1707), 47, 56-59

Arnstadt Consistory, 56-57, 58n.

Art of Fugue, The (1748-1750), 43, 68

Asenath, wife of Joseph (Gen. 41:45), 89

Ashtabula (Ohio), 159

Athalia (1733), 82

Athanasian Creed (*Quicunque vult*), 24

Attilio, 78

Augustine, Saint (354-430), 4, 8-9, 21

Augustus II of Saxony (1670-1733; known as "the Strong"), 59-62

Augustus III of Saxony (1696-1763), 62-64

Austin, John (1613-1669)
Reformed Devotions compiled from, 117
author of Devotions In the Antient Way of Offices (Paris, 1668), 118
"fondling expressions" in his hymns, 119
hymns not inspected by any "proper judicature," 123

Bach, Carl Philipp Emanuel (1714-1788), third son of J. S. Bach, 61

Bach, Catharina Dorothea (1708-1774), eldest daughter of J. S. Bach, 70

Bach, Johann Sebastian (1685-1750), 41-77
born at Eisenach, 12
death, circumstances of, 43
sacred works more frequently performed in concert hall than Handel's oratorios, 92
Samuel Wesley's regard for, 136
usefulness of (evangelistic meetings), 151-152

Bainton, R. H., 10n.

Barnes, Robert (1495-1540), protestant martyr, 33n.

Baxter, Richard (1615-1691), hymnist and nonconformist leader, 93

Bay Psalm Book (1640), first book published in English colonies, 20

Beethoven, Ludwig van (1770-1827), 91-92

"Before Jehovah's Awful Throne" (Watts's Psalm C), 121

Belshazzar (d. 539 B.C.; Baby-lonian general, son of Nabonidos), 87

Belshazzar (Handel's oratorio, 1745), 87, 89

Benedict XV, Pope (1854-1922), 165, 170

Benson, Louis F. (1855-1930), 118n., 120n.

Berlin, Irving (b. 1888), 182

Bernard of Clairvaux, Saint (1091-1153), 74

Bernard of Morlaix (preferably of Cluny; fl. 1145; author of De Contemptu Mundi), 150

Bernstein, Leonard (b. 1918), 183n.

Bett, Henry, 125n.

Beza, Theodore (1519-1605), Calvinist divine, 20

"Black Rubric" (1552 Prayer-book), 28

Blasius, Saint, Church of (Mül-hausen), 47

Bliss, Philip Paul (1838-1876), 153n., 159, 162

Bloch, Ernest (b. 1880), 182

Bonar, Horatius (1808-1889), 156

Bononcini, Giovanni Battista (1672-1750), 78, 83

Booke of Common Praier noted (1550), 24-40

Booke of Notes and Common-places (1581), 38-39

Bourgeois, Louis (b. 1510?; choirmaster at Geneva; 1541-1557; probable composer of 85 tunes in Genevan psalters, including tune now known as Old Hundredth; last heard of at Paris in 1561, where he published harmonizations of the Genevan psalter melodies), 19-20

Boyce, William (1770-1779), 131
Boyd, John, S.J., 175
Bradbury, William B. (1816-1868; compiler of 59 singing books), 154
Bradford, Gamaliel, 153n., 161n.
Brattle, Thomas (1658-1713; Boston merchant), 17
Bray, Thomas (1656-1730; influential in founding of Society for the Promotion of Christian Knowledge), associates of, 126
Brennan, Robert E., Msgr., 170-172
Bridges, Robert (1844-1930; poet laureate), 19
"Brief Life Is Here Our Portion" (Bernard of Cluny, 1145), 140
Bristol, Charles Wesley's residence at, 131
British Museum, Samuel Wesley manuscripts in, 138
Britt, Matthew, O.S.B., 150n.
Broughton, Thomas (1712-1777), 120
Browning, Robert (1812-1889), 77
Bryant, William Cullen (1794-1878), use of his hymns in Union Hymnal, 180
Bucer, Martin (1491-1551; Alsatian reformer), 4, 28
Buchanan, Duncan, 171
Bünting, Heinrich (Itinerarium Sacrae Scripturae, 1585), 75
Bukofzer, Manfred (b. 1910), 37n., 54n.
Bullinger, Henry (1504-1575; Swiss reformer), 4, 27
Burney, Charles (1726-1814; pioneer music historian), erroneous birthdate for Merbecke, 30
George III's fondness for Handel, 81
opinion of Messiah overture, 89
opinion of J. S. Bach, 136
Burns, Robert (1759-1796), 135n.
Buszin, Walter E., 5n.
Byrd, William (1543-1643), 138
Byrnes, Aquinas, O.P., 150

Caecilia: A Catholic Review of Musical Art, 169, 174n.
Calvin, John (1509-1564), 4, 10, 13-23, 31 (epistle against "Six Articles"), 35, 44
Calvinism, enmity against (18th-century Leipzig), 48
Calvinist disapproval: of solo singing, 156; of organs, 157
Calvisius, Seth (1556-1615; Leipzig cantor), 50
Cambridge, Samuel Wesley's visit to, 133
Canaan, 97
Canada, French church music in, 172
Cannons (Handel hymn-tune), 134
cantata[s]
Bach's five-year cycle of, 44
use of (18th-century Leipzig), 51
orthodoxy in Bach's cycle of, 52-53
"cant expressions" in the Wesley 1780 hymnbook, Neale's criticism of, 147-148
cantorate at Leipzig, 42, 46, 65, 67
capellmeister, post of, 46, 65

Carlstadt, Andreas Bodenstein of (1480-1541), 4
Carson, Alexander, 73n.
castrati
    in Italian opera, 78
    in English oratorio, 81, 89
Catechism Preludes (1739: *Clavierübung*, Vol. III), 54
Catholic Choirmaster, 150n., 169
Causton, Thomas (Wesley's opponent in Georgia), 117-118
Central Conference of American Rabbis, 177
Central Synagogue (New York City), 178
Chalmers Memorial Free Church (Edinburgh), 156
Chandos, Duke of (Brydges, James [1673-1744]), 79-80
Chapel Royal
    boy choristers from, 80
    organs removed from, 16
    religious indifferentism in (Elizabeth's), 33n.
Charleston, South Carolina
    Wesley's first *Collection of Psalms and Hymns* printed at, 114
    Wesley's first visit to, 127
    Wesley's second visit to, 127n.
Charlestown Collection (1737)
    borrowings from Austin and Hickes, 118
    borrowings from Watts, 120
    "first real Anglican hymnal," 116
    items carried over into 1784 *Collection*, 114-115
chazzan (cantor in a synagogue), 185n.
Chicago, Moody's beginnings at, 155

Chichester, Bishop of, 142-143
    see Gilbert, Ashurst Turner
China, evangelical hymnals published in, 159
choirs, training of, 10
chorale, Bach's last composition, 55
chorales
    singing of (Reform temple at Hamburg), 185
    treasury of (used by Bach), 49
"Christ Dying, Interceding, and Reigning" (Watts's Psalm II), 94
"Christian, Dost Thou See Them" (Andrew of Crete [660-732]), 141
Christian Remembrancer, Neale's 1849 (October) article in, 146-148
Christliche Geseng Lateinisch und Deutsch, zum Begrebnis, 6
Christmas carols, devotional expression in, 175n.
Christmas Oratorio (1734), 44, 67
"Christ's All-Sufficiency" (Watt's Psalm XVI), 94
Church of England, hymn singing an innovation in, 116
Church of England in Canada (1938 hymnal), 159
Cibber, Susanna Maria, Mrs. (1714-1766; contralto and dramatic actress), 85
Cibber, Theophilus (married Susanna in 1734), 85
Cicero, 73, 76
Civil War, Sankey's role in, 154
Clavierübung, Bach's (Vol. II, 1735; Vol. III, 1739), 77

Cleopatra, daughter of Ptolemy Philometor (I Macc. 10: 57), 90
Clifford, William Kingdon, Professor (1845-1879), 158
Cöthen, Bach's career at (1717-1723), 44-46
Coke, Thomas, Dr. (1747-1814; Wesley's coadjutor), 115
Coleridge, Samuel Taylor (1772-1834), 125
Collected Hymns, Sequences, and Carols (Neale), 140n.
Collection of Psalms and Hymns (Wesley, 1737), see *Charlestown Collection*
Collection of Psalms and Hymns (Wesley, 1738)
  first collection published in England, 114
  three surviving copies of, 129
Collection of Psalms and Hymns (Wesley brothers, 1784), 114
Collection of Psalms and Hymns (Wesley brothers, 1784), last publication specifically designed for Methodist Societies, 114-115
Colman, Benjamin, Dr. (1673-1747; Boston divine), 100
"Colonies Planted: A Psalm for New England" (Watts's Psalm CVII), 99
"Come Holy Spirit, Send Down Those Beams" (Austin hymn preserved by John Wesley), 119
"Come, Thou Almighty King," 180
concordance, Latin, 36
concordance, Merbecke's (first in English, 1550), 29-30 31n., 35-36
Concordia Formula, 74

Conference between the Pope and his Secretary (1582), 40
"Congreso Internacional de Música Sagrada" (Rome, 1950), 176n.
Copland, Aaron (b. 1900), 182
Cotton, John (1585-1652), 17
Coverdale, Miles (1488-1568), 124
Cowley, Abraham (1618-1667), 95
Cowper, William (1731-1800)
  "heresy" in his hymns criticized by Neale, 146, 148
  hymns in *Union Hymnal*, 180
Cram, Ralph Adams (b. 1863), 168-169
Cranmer, Thomas, Archbishop (1489-1556), 25-26
Crashaw, Richard (1613?-1649), 104n.
Creation, The (1798), 121
Credo (Lutheran liturgy), 49
Croft, William (1678-1727), 180
Cromwell, Oliver (1599-1658), destruction of organs under, 16
Cromwell, Thomas (1485?-1540), 40
Curnock, Nehemiah, 113n., 132n.
Cyropaedia (Xenophon), 87
Cyrus, Persian King, 87, 89

Dafne, earliest German opera (Schütz, 1627), 11
Dagon, Philistine deity, 88
Dali, Salvador (b. 1904), 174
Dalyell, Sir John Graham (1776-1851; Scottish antiquary), 17n.
dancing, the "chiefest mischiefe of all" (quotation from Calvin), 22n.

Daniel
  role in Handel's *Belshazzar*,
    sung by male contralto, 89
  Book of, 87
Dannreuther, Edward (1844-
  1905; music historian),
  133, 137
Danzig, 48
Darius (558?-485 B.C.; fourth
  king of Persia), 87
Dark Night of the Soul, The
  (poem by St. John of the
  Cross), 113
David, second King of Israel,
  "cloudy Jewishness of," 94
  made to speak like an 18th-
    century Britisher, 96
  preferred above Watts, 99
  Watts's complaints against,
    100-101
David, Hans. T. (b. 1902; mu-
  sicologist), 57n., 69n.
Davis, Arthur P., 104n.
*Day of Judgment, an Ode, in
  English Sapphic* (Watts),
  103
Dearmer, Percy (1867-1936;
  English hymnologist; canon
  of Westminster), 93n. 141
De Doctrina Christiana (Milton's
  Arian treatise), 144
Deidamia (Handel's last opera,
  1741), 79
De La Warr, Lord, 143
  see West, George John
Demetrius II (called "Nicator";
  king of Syria: I Macc.
  7:1-6; 10:1, 47-50), 90
De Profundis, penitential psalm,
  110
Des Prés, Josquin (1450?-1521;
  greatest Netherlands com-
  poser of his generation), 5
*Deudsche Messe und Ordnung
  Gottis Diensts* (German lit-

urgy, framed during 1525
  by Luther, assisted by
  Johann Walther and Con-
  rad Rupff, for optional use
  in place of the Latin liturgy), 7-8
Devotions (Hickes, used by Wesley while in Georgia), 117-
  118, 119n.
Deyling, Salomo, Dr. (1677-
  1755; Lutheran divine, and
  superintendent at Leip-
  zig), 54
*Dialogue between Youth and
  Olde Age, A* (1584), 39
Diaries, Wesley's, written in cipher, 112-113
Dies Irae (attributed to Thomas
  of Celano, 13th century,
  words based on Zeph. 1:14-
  15, and music taken from
  Respond sung at Absolution
  of the Dead), 148
Directory of Worship (Presbyterian Church, U.S.A.), 18
Discourses, Essays, and Tracts
  (Watts, 1753), 107n.
Divine and Moral Songs (Watts,
  1715; prepared for use of,
  and dedicated to, his youthful pupils, Sarah, Mary,
  and Elizabeth Abney), 103
Divini Cultus (Pius XI, 1928),
  170
Doane, William Howard (1832-
  1915), 159
Doddridge, Philip (1702-1751;
  hymnist and Independent
  clergyman), 95n.
Donne, John (1573-1631; poet,
  divine, and dean of St.
  Paul's), 93
Douen, Orentin, 19, 21
Douglas, Winfred (1867-1944;
  hymnologist and editor,

The Hymnal 1940), 19n., 25n., 116n.
"Dragon of Rome," Merbecke's polemic against, 40
Dramma per musica (Leipzig, 1727), 61
Dresden, 59, 64
Drinker, H. S., 52n.
Dryden, John (1631-1700), 95, 96n., 102
Dublin (*Messiah* première, 1742), 84-85
Dunlap, C. H., Rev., 160
Dykes, J. B. (1823-1876; clergyman and composer of several enormously successful hymn-tunes), 141

East Grinstead (England), 143
Edinburgh, Moody and Sankey at, 156-157
Edward VI, King (reigned 1547-1553)
decree abolishing organ playing at Windsor, 39
injunction against organs, 16
Sternhold and Hopkins metrical psalter compiled during reign of, 116
Edwardine Prayerbook (1549)
Hickes's preference for, 117
Wesley's use of (in Georgia), 118
Egmont, Earl of (Perceval, John [1683-1748]), 80
Egypt
plagues depicted musically, 82
Sankey's visit to, 154
Ein' Feste Burg (Luther's metrical paraphrase of Psalm 46, published in approximately 1529, and thereafter "Battle Hymn of the Reformation"; first translated into English in Coverdale's *Goostly Psalmes*, 1539), 45
Einstein, Alfred (1880-1952; musicologist), 41, 52n.
Eisenach, Bach's birthplace, 12
Elijah (Mendelssohn's second oratorio; first performed, Birmingham, 1846), 51
Ellard, Gerald, S. J., 170n.
Ellerton, John (1826-1893), 180
Emerson, Ralph Waldo (1803-1882), 125
Emmett, Daniel D. (1815-1904; composer of *Dixie*), 162
"English Hymnology: Its History and Prospects" (Neale), 146-148, 149n.
Episcopal Hymnal, *see* Protestant Episcopal Hymnal
Erba, Dionigi (17th-century maestro di cappella at Milan, and reputedly composer of a double-choir *Magnificat* refurbished by Handel for use in *Israel in Egypt*), 83
Erdmann, Georg (Russian agent at Danzig), 48
Ernesti, Johann August (1707-1781), 64, 68-77
Ernesti, Sophie (daughter of Johann August), 76-77
Escorial, El (Spain), 176n.
Estey organ, Sankey's use of, 156
Esther (Handel's first English oratorio), 79-81
Eton College, destruction of musical archive at, 38
Eucharist, music for, 29
Exeter College, 120

Farel, William (1485-1565; Swiss reformer, and precursor of Calvin at Geneva), 4

Fauré, Gabriel (1845-1924), 22

Fellowes, E. H. (1870-1951), 29n.

Fénelon, François de Salignac (1651-1715; French prelate), 135n.

figural music, Bach's failure to perform, 57

"figured music," Cranmer's objection to, 25

Filmer, Henry, 32-33

financing of church music, Luther's plan, 10

FitzGerald, Edward (1809-1883), 79n.

Fitzwilliam (hymn-tune by Handel), 134

"Fix'd in His Everlasting Seat" (*Samson*), 88

Flower, Sir Newman, 81n., 87n.

"fondling expressions" addressed to Divinity, Watts's use of, 104-106

Fortunatus, Venantius (530-609; bishop of Poitiers), 150

"For Unto Us a Child Is Born" (*Messiah*), 83

Foster, Stephen Collins (1826-1864), 154, 162

Found[e]ry, tunes used at (1742), 121n.

Foundling Hospital (London), established for exposed and deserted children in 1739, 86

Foxe, John (1516-1587; martyrologist), 32, 33n. 34, 36n.

Franck, César (1822-1890), 137

Francke, A. H. (1663-1727; divine, professor at Halle, and philanthropist), 51n., 125

Franklin, Benjamin (1706-1790), 126, 128

Frauenkirche (Dresden), 63

Frederick (II) the Great (1712-1786; Prussian king), 67

Free Church College (Edinburgh), 156

Frere, W. H., 24n.

Freud, Sigmund (1856-1939), 104

Friedländer, David (1750-1834), 184

Fuller Maitland, J. A. (1856-1936), opinions of concerning Wesleys' musical talents, 137

Gabrieli, Andrea (1510?-1586), 50

Gabrieli, Giovanni (1557-1612; son of Andrea), 50

Gardiner, Stephen (1493?-1555; bishop of Winchester), 34-37

Garret, Protestant martyr, 33n.

Garside, Charles, 23n.

Gaudlitz, Gottlieb (Leipzig clergyman; pastor of St. Thomas Church, 1741-1745), 54

Gay, John (1685-1732), 78-79

General Convention (Protestant Episcopal Church), 149

Geneva
Calvin's influence at, 18-19
Town Council, minutes of, 16

Genevan Service Book of 1556, 21

Gentile organists and singers, role of (Reform temples), 183

George I (reigned 1714-1727), pension granted Handel by, 81n.

George II (reigned 1727-1760), coronation music for, 82
Handel pensioned by, 81n.

lauded by Watts ("royal saint"), 98
George III (reigned 1760-1820) stands during "Hallelujah Chorus", 81 recognizes talents of Charles Wesley the Younger, 133
Georgia (Wesley's sojourn) difficult months in, 112 Hickes and Thomas à Kempis favored as devotional reading, 117 selection of hymns for use in, 114
Gerber, C. G. (1660-1731), 54n.
Gerhardt, Paul (1607-1676; greatest German hymnist after Luther), 62
German hymns in translation, 124-125
Gershwin, George (1898-1937), 182
Geystliche Gesangk Buchleyn (1524), 8
Giardini, Felice de (1716-1796), 180
Gibson, Edmund (1669-1748; bishop of London), 80, 82
Gilbert, Ashurst Turner, Bishop (1786-1870), 142-143
Gladstone, William (1809-1898), 152
Glasgow Presbytery, vote against organs taken by (1807), 17
Gloria (Lutheran liturgy), 49
"Glorious Things of Thee Are Spoken" (Newton, 1779), 148
Glory of Christ as God-Man (Arian treatise), 107
Gluck, Christoph Willibald (1714-1787), 91
Gobryas (Xenophon's Anabasis I:7-12), 87

God and the Bible (Matthew Arnold), quotation from, 157-158
Görner, Johann Gottlieb (1697-1778; organist at St. Paul's [University] Church, Leipzig, 1721; organist at St. Thomas's, 1729), 60
Goethe, Johann Wolfgang von (1749-1832), 73
Goldberg, Johann Gottlieb (harpsichordist, pupil of Bach: 1733-1746), see Goldberg Variations
Goldberg Variations (Aria with 30 Variations, 1742), 63n., 67, 69, 77
Golding, Arthur (1536?-1605?), 22n.
Goldmark, Carl (1832-1915), 182
Goostly Psalmes and Spirituall Songes (ca. 1539), 124
Gopsal (Handel hymn-tune), 134n.
Gospel for the Day, 24, 50, 52
"Gospel hymns," derivation of, 158
Goudimel, Claude (1505-1572), 20n.
Gounod, Charles François (1818-1893), 173
Grant, Sir Robert (1779-1838; jurist and hymn-writer), 180
Graupner, Christoph (1683-1760), 42
Gray, Cecil, 41n.
Great Awakening (1740-1745), 95
Green, Richard, 115n.
Gregorian chant (see also plainsong)
Merbecke's revisions of, 27

Neale's fondness for, 140
practical difficulties inhibiting use of, 172, 175
"peculiar treasure" of Catholic Church, 167, 170
Samuel Wesley's interest in, 135
Gude and Godlie Ballates (*ca.* 1550; 2nd edition, 1567), 124
Gunpowder Plot, 104

Haggai, 86
Halévy, Jacques F. F. (1799-1862), 182
Hall, Edward, 34-35
Halle, 12, 47, 125
"Hallelujah Chorus" (*Messiah*), 85
Haman and Mordecai (1720), 79
Hamburg, Reform temple in (founded 1817), 184
Hamor, fictitious warrior-hero in Handel's *Jephtha*, 89
Handel, George Frideric (1685-1759), 78-92
    appeal of, compared with Sankey's 153
    born in Halle, 12
    darling of 19th-century British musical public, 134
    hymn-tunes borrowed for use in *Union Hymnal*, 180
    hymn-tunes composed for Charles Wesley's stanzas, 134
    "Joy to the World" ascribed to, but without warrant, 100
    oratorios not presented in church, but in concert-hall, 51
Handel Festival of 1784, 81
"Happy Soul, Thy Days Are Ended" (Wesleyan hymn-book, 1800), 147
"Hark! the Herald Angels Sing" (1739, adapted), 150
harmony singing, prohibition against, 21
Harris, Roy (b. 1898), 175n.
Hartford, University of, 148-149
Harvard University, 148
Harvard University hymnbook, 53
Hatfield, James T., 124n., 125
Hawkins, Sir John (1719-1789), 31n., 33n., 34n., 35n., 36n., 38n.
    opinions on *Messiah* airs, 89
Haydn, Franz Josef (1732-1809), 91, 121
Haydn, Johann Michael (1737-1806; composer of music for "O Worship the King"), 180
Hayes, Philip, Dr. (1738-1797; professor of music at Oxford), 131n.
Heine, Heinrich (1797-1856), 185
"He Leadeth Me" (1862), 154
Henry V, musical accomplishments of, 37n.
Henry VIII (reigned 1509-1547)
    attempt to halt Protestant influences, 30
    Cranmer's letter to, 25
    performer on lute and organ; composer, 37
    "sympathy" for his victims, 36n.
Herbert, George (1593-1632), 93, 123
heresy in hymns, Neale's fear of, 146, 148-150
hermeneutics, science of Scripture interpretation, 72

Herrick, Robert (1591-1674), 93

"He Was Despised and Rejected of Men" (*Messiah*), 85

Hickes, George (1642-1715; nonjuring divine), 117, 119, 123

Higginson, J. Vincent, 150n.

Hippodrome (New York), 1875 Christian Convention at, 153

"His Yoke Is Easy" (*Messiah*), 83

"Hold the Fort, For I Am Coming" (P. P. Bliss), 152-153

Holy Communion, music for, 28

"Holy, Holy, Holy" (music by Dykes), 139

Homer, 53, 101-102

Hooper, John, Bishop (b. 1555), 27

Horae Lyricae (1706), 103-104

Housman, A. E., 111

How, William Walsham, Bishop (1823-1897), 180

"How Sweet the Name of Jesus Sounds" (Newton, 1774), 148

Huguenots, psalter used by, 22n.

humaniora, music not allowed to compete with, 69

Humbert (Crown Prince of Italy), 156

Hume, Paul Chandler (Washington music critic), 173-174

Hunt, J. Eric, 34n.

Hunter College (New York City), 169n.

Huycke, 21

Hymnal 1940 Companion, 148, 150n.

"hymns of human composure," objection to, 13

Hymns Ancient and Modern (Historical Edition, 1909), 141, 143

Hymns and Spiritual Songs . . . With an Essay Towards the Improvement of Christian Psalmody (Watts, 1707), 93; 94n., 103

Hymns for Children (Neale, 1842), 145

Hymns of the Breviary and Missal, The (ed. Matthew Britt), 150

Hymns of the Dominican Missal and Breviary (ed. Aquinas Byrnes), 150n.

Hymns of the Eastern Church (Neale, 1866), 140n.

Hymns of Prayer and Praise, 158-159

"Hymn to Christ" (Hymn XXXVIII in Wesley's 1737 *Collection*), 119

"Hymn to the Name and Honour of the Admirable Saint Teresa" (Crashaw), 104n.

"I Am Praying For You" (Sankey), 151

Idelsohn, A. Z. (1882-1938), 179, 181n., 185n.

Iliad, 53, 103n.

"I'll Praise My Maker While I've Breath" (Watts's Psalm CXLVI), 122

"imitation," theories of, 95-96

"Inconstancy" (Wesley *Collection*, 1737), 119

indices, lack of (Austin, Hickes, and early Wesley collections), 119n.

inhibition, Neale's, 142-144

innovations, Bach's, resentment against, 57

Institutio Interpretis N. T., 72

instrumental music (in church) Calvin's injunctions against, 15

Merbecke's polemic against, 39

"senseless and absurd aping"

of figurative Old Testament worship, 14-15
tolerated in man's spiritual infancy, 14
introits, singing of (Leipzig), 50
Iphis, Jephthah's daughter, 89
Isaiah
verses from, used in *Belshazzar*, 87
verses from, used in *Messiah*, 86
Ishmael, 66
Israel in Egypt (1739), 82, 87
Israel Symphony Orchestra, 184
"It Passeth Knowledge," 152

Jacopo da Bologna (*fl.* 1350), 175n.
Japan, evangelical hymnals published in, 159
Jehovah's contest with Dagon, 88
Jennens, Charles (1700-1773)
calls *Messiah* "Entertainment," 84
librettist for *Belshazzar*, 87
librettist for *Saul* and *Messiah*, 82
"vain fool crazed by his wealth," 86
Jennings, David, Dr. (1691-1762; dissenting divine), 95n.
Jephtha (1752), 88, 90
Jephthah (Judg. 11:1-34), 88
"*Jeremiah*" *Symphony* (Bernstein, 1944), 183
Jericho, 88
Jerome, 33n.
Jeroboam, 32
Jerusalem, 59
"Jerusalem the Golden" (Bernard of Cluny, 1145), 140
"Jesu, Behold the Wise from Far" (Austin hymn in 1737 *Charlestown Collection*), 119
"Jesus, Lover of My Soul" (1740), 105, 130, 147
"Jesus Shall Reign Where'er the Sun" (Watts's Psalm LXXII)), 100
Jewish ancestry, Mendelssohn's reference to, 65
Jewish congregations, autonomy of, 178n.
Jewish Music in Its Historical Development (1929), 180
Joacim (Sus. 1:1, 4, 6, 63), 89
Job, Book of, 86
Job, Sermons on (Calvin), 22
John the Steadfast (1468-1532; Elector of Saxony), 11
Johnson, Samuel, Dr. (1709-1784), 86, 101-102, 111, 123, 147
Jonathan, friend of David, 90
Jordan river, 88
Joseph, 89
Joseph and His Brethren (1744), 89
Joshua (1748), 67, 88, 91
Journals (John Wesley)
correction of misleading statements in, 115
notice of attendance at nephew's recital, 132
"Joy to the World" (Watts's Psalm XCVIII), 100, 134n.
Joys and Glories of Paradise (1865), 140n.
Judaism in America, divisions of, 177
Judas Maccabaeus (1747), 67, 90
"Just As I Am" (Charlotte Elliott, 1836), 139, 154

Kahnis, C. F. A., 73n., 74n.

Kant, Immanuel (1724-1804), 161
Kayserling, Carl Freiherr von (Russian envoy at Dresden), 63-64
Kempis, Thomas à (1380-1471), 117, 135n.
Ken, Thomas (1637-1711; bishop of Bath and Wells), 93
King's Chapel (Boston), 17
Kinnoull, Lord (Hay, George [d. 1758]), 84
"kist o' whistles" (contemptuous Scots term for an organ), 156
Knox, John (1505?-1572), 156
Köhler, J. F. (pastor of Taucha, near Leipzig, and author of *Historia Scholarum Lipsiensium*, 1776), 69
Kol Nidre (Schönberg, 1938), 185
Krause
  Gottfried Theodor, senior prefect dismissed by Ernesti, 69-70
  Johann Gottlieb, replacement for the preceding (1736), 71
Kuhnau, Johann (1660-1722; Leipzig cantor after 1701), 59, 61
Kunst der Fuge, Die, 43, 68
Kyrie (Lutheran liturgy), 50

La Ciudad de Dios, quotation from, 176n.
LaFarge, John, S.J. (editor of *America*), 171, 172n.
Lambeth Conferences, music at, 29
Lamentations, Book of, 86
Lang, P. H. (b. 1901; musicologist), 173
La Rue, Pierre de (d. 1518;

Netherlands contrapuntist), 5
La Scala Opera House (Milan), 175
Lassus, Orlandus (1530/2-1594), 11
Latin music, Merbecke's 38
Latin school-texts, Ernesti's, 72
Law, William, nonjuror, 112
Lawrence, owner of copyright on Watts's 1707 *Hymns*, 109
"Lead, Kindly Light" (Newman, 1833; music by Dykes, 1865), 141
Lee, Umphrey, 113, 135n.
Leichtentritt, Hugo (b. 1874; musicologist), 41n.
Leipzig
  church music in (18th century), 42, 46
  population during 1730's, 49
Leipzig Consistory, 62, 64, 71, 76
Leipzig Interim, 49
Leipzig period, Bach's activities during (1723-1750), 59, 61, 67
Leipzig Town Council, 42, 48, 62, 64, 71
Leipzig University, 46, 60-61, 70
Lenox Collection (New York Public Library), 129
Leo XIII, Pope (1810-1903), 176
Leopold of Anhalt-Cöthen, Prince, 44-45
Levites (temple singers), 14
Lightwood, James T., 131n.
Liszt, Franz (1811-1886), 137
Litany of 1544 (Cranmer), 25
liturgy
  Bach's devotion to, 53
  English, 29

Latin (18th-century Leipzig), 49
vernacular, 7, 14
Wesley accused of inverting order of, and method, 117
Longfellow, Samuel (1819-1892), 180
Lotario (1729), 79
Lotti, Antonio (1667-1740; Venetian composer), 83
Lowell, James Russell (1819-1891), 180
Lowrie, Walter, 159n.
lute
  Luther as performer on, 8
  Henry VIII as performer on, 37
Luther, Martin (1483-1546), 3-12
  Bach's indebtedness to, 49
  Bach's role in interpreting, 52
  Shorter Catechism of, 54
  works of (in Bach's library), 46

Maccabees, Books of, 90-91
Magnalia Christi Americana (Cotton Mather, 1702), 17
Magnificat (Bach, 1723), 45, 67
Malachi, 86
Mahler, Gustav (1860-1911), 182
Mahomet, 128
Manhattanville College of the Sacred Heart, 168
Mantua (Italy), 167, 182
Manual of Presbyterian Law (1947), 18
Marot, Clément (1496-1544), 19-20
Marienkirche (Mülhausen), opposition to Pietism at, 47
Marshalsea prison, Merbecke's term in, 34

Mary (the Blessed Virgin Mary), 32, 38
Marylebone, Charles Wesley's residence at, 131
Maskell, William (1814-1890), 25n.
Mass
  High, 28n., 50
  Low (elimination of music at), 174
Mass in B Minor (Bach), 51, 62-64, 67
Masses, Short (Bach: A, F, G Major and G Minor), 69
Mass, for boys' and men's voices and ten instruments (Stravinsky, 1948), 175
Mather, Cotton (1663-1728), 17
Matheus de Perusio, 175n.
Matthews, Thomas (pseudonym for John Rogers), 31
Matisse, Henri (b. 1869), 174
Maynard, Theodore, 169n.
Maxwell, William D., 13n., 21, 20n.
McMillan, William, 16n.
McMurtrie, Douglas C., 126n., 127n.
Mediator Dei (1947), 165, 170-171, 174, 176
Mendel, Arthur (b. 1905), 57n., 69n.
Mendelssohn, Felix (1809-1847)
  Elijah not written for church presentation, 51
  St. Matthew Passion revived by (Berlin, 1829), 65
  Samuel Wesley's sacred music compared, 137
  wrote no specifically "Jewish" music, 182
Merab, Saul's daughter, 90
Messiah (1742), 78-79, 82-89
  borrowings from earlier Italian works, 83

composed in twenty-four days
(1741), 78
most frequently performed of
Handel's oratorios, 67, 91
offensive to the pious, because
an "Entertainment," 84
words by Charles Jennens, 82
Methodism, dates for unfolding
of (supplied by Wesley),
115-116
Methodist hymnal, 129 (first),
139, 159, 178n. (obligatory
use of)
Methodist tunebook (1742),
first, 121
"Methodistical hymnizing," 145
Mexico, evangelical hymnals
published in, 159
Meyerbeer, Giacomo (1791-
1864), 182
Michael, identified with Christ
by Watts, 107-108
Milton, John (1608-1674), 87,
144
modes, use of (Deudsche Messe),
7
Moffatt, James, quoted, 144-145
Montgomery, James (1771-
1854), 180
Moody, Dwight L. (1837-1899),
152-158, 160-161
Moravian hymns, 148
Moravians
Wesley's associations with, 124
Zinzendorf's leadership, 125
Morning Hymn Book, The
(Coke), 115
Mosheim, Johann Lorenz von
(1693-1755), 72
Moses, 94, 169
Moses, Rabbi Isaac, 178
motets (Latin), singing of (at
Leipzig), 50
Motu Proprio (1903), 165-166,
168, 170-171

Mozart, W. A. (1756-1791),
22, 131
Mülhausen, Bach's career at
(1707-1708), 43, 47, 56,
58-59
Müller, Heinrich (1631-1675;
author of Himmlischer Lie-
beskuss), 75
Munich, 11
music education, obligatory
in Lutheran schools, 7
in seminaries, 7
misprints, Luther's care against,
9
Musical Offering (Bach, 1747),
58, 69, 77
Music of the Roman Rite, The
(R. R. Terry), 39
Myers, Robert Manson, 81n.,
89n.
My Life and the Story of Gospel
Hymns (Sankey), 160
mysticism, Bach's leanings toward, 47

Naumann, Emil (1827-1888),
11n.
Neale, John Mason (1818-
1866), 139-150
Neander, Joachim (1650-1680),
142
"Nearer, My God, to Thee"
(Sarah F. Adams, 1841),
139
Nef, Karl (b. 1873), 53n.
Netherlands contrapuntists, Lu-
ther's fondness for, 9
Nettl, Paul (b. 1889), 5n., 9n.,
182n.
Neumark, Georg (1621-1681),
180
New Castle (Pennsylvania),
Sankey's associations with,
155, 160

New England, A Psalm for (Watts), 99

New York *Herald-Tribune*, 184

Newman, John Henry, Cardinal (1801-1890), 141

Newton, John (1725-1807), 148

Nicolaikirche (St. Nicholas Church, Leipzig), 43, 61

nonjurors, 117

Novello, Vincent (1781-1861), 135

"O Bless His Name, Ye Britons" (Watts's Psalm CIV), 98

"O Britain, Praise Thy Mighty God" (Watts's Psalm CXLVII), 98

"O God, Thou Bottomless Abyss" (Hymn XVI in 1737 *Collection*), 125

"O Worship the King," 180

Odyssey, 103n.

Offenbach, Jacques (1819-1880), 182

Oglethorpe, James (1696-1785; founder of Georgia colony), attends concert given by John Wesley's nephews, 132n.

Oking, Robert (*fl.* 1525-1554; archdeacon of Salisbury), 36

Olearius, Johann Christoph (1668-1747; superintendent at Arnstadt), 57

Old Hall Manuscript, 37n.

Olivers, Thomas, 179

Ollard, S. L., 37n.

Olney Hymns, 148

"Onward, Christian Soldiers" (S. Baring-Gould, 1864), 140

operas of Handel, modern revivals of, 91

organ

Geneva, melting of, 15

Hamburg, use of (Reform temple), 184-185

organ playing, standards of (Catholic churches), 169

organs

Calvin's antagonism toward, 13

Luther's favorable attitude, 10

New England, introduction into, 17

Scotland, destruction of, 17

Original Sequences, Hymns, and Other Ecclesiastical Verses (Neale, 1866), 146

Orthodox Judaism, organs banned in, 178

orthodoxy, Lutheran (18th century), 43-44

Othniel (*Joshua*), 88

"Our God, Our Help in Ages Past" (Watts's Psalm XC), 111n., 140, 180

Ovid (*Epistles*), 95

Oxford

rise of Methodism at (1729), 115

music degree from, 133

Oxford History of Music, 26, 133, 137

Oxford University, destruction of music library at, 38

Palestine, Sankey's visit to, 154

Palestrina, Giovanni Pierluigi da (1525-1594), 22

Partenope (1730), 79

Pascal, Blaise (1623-1662), 135n.

Patrick, Millar, 144

Paul, Apostle, 59

enjoins prayer and praise in "known tongue," 15

Paulinerkirche (University Church at Leipzig), 60

Passion According to St. John, see *St. John Passion*

Passion According to St. Matthew, see *St. Matthew Passion*

Pepusch, John Christopher (1667-1752), 79

Person, Anthony, 32-33

Peterkin, Alexander (1780-1846), 16

Pfeiffer, August (1640-1698; archdeacon, St. Thomas Church, Leipzig, 1681; orientalist and professor at Leipzig University), 46, 74

Pharaoh, 89, 169

Philadelphia Library Society, 126

Philistines, 90

Phillips, Robert, 33

Pietism, 18th-century, 47-48, 125

Pietists, attitude toward music, 54

Pious Communicant Rightly Prepared, The (Samuel Wesley, 1700), 120

Pius VI, Pope (1717-1799), 135

Pius X, Pope (1835-1914), 165-170, 183

Pius XI, Pope (1857-1939), 165

Pius XII, Pope (b. 1876), 165, 170, 174, 176

Pius X School of Liturgical Music, 168

plagiarism, Handel accused of, 82-83

plainsong (plainchant)
  adaptation to English of Latin repertory, 27
  lessons sung in, 24-25
  simplest melodies favored by Cranmer, 26
  singing of common in, 172

Poland, 59

Pope, Alexander (1688-1744), 101-102

Portuguese Chapel . (London), music at, 134-135

Potiphera[h], priest of On (Gen. 41:45), 89

Poulenc, François (b. 1899), 175n.

Praetorius, Michael (1572-1621), 8

Prayer Book Dictionary (Harford and Stevenson), 27

prayers for the dead, music for, 28

Presbyterian Church (US), opposition to hymns in, 21

Presbyterian Hymnal (*The Hymnal*, 1933), 139

Preuss, Hans, 74n.

Procter, Francis, 24n.

"Promise and Sign of Christ's Coming" (Watts's Psalm XIII), 94

"promises" in Old and New Testament, Watts's contrasting of, 97

Protestant Episcopal Church (USA)
  "heretical" hymns used by, 149
  The Hymnal 1940, 139
  The Hymnal 1940 Companion, 150
  use of Merbecke's music in, 29

Prunières, Henry (b. 1886), 4 1n.

Prussia, 67

Psalms, Calvin's exegesis of, 71, 92

psalms in meter
  Neale's dislike of accepted versions of, 147
  obligatory singing of, 13
  singing of (Cöthen), 45

Watts's version, 100-101
Psalms of David Imitated in the
    Language of the New
    Testament (Watts, 1719),
    93-94, 100
Ptolemy Philometor (181-145
    B.C. [I Macc. 10:51-58]),
    90
"Pull for the Shore, Sailor" (P.
    P. Bliss), 159
Purcell, Henry (1659-1695),
    135n.
Puritans and music, 38

Quicunque vult (Athanasian
    Creed), 24
Rambach, Johann Jakob (1693-
    1735; author of Betrach-
    tung über den Rath Gottes
    von der Schlechtigkeit der
    Menschen and Betrachtung
    der Thränen und Seuffzer
    Jesu Christi), 75
Ratzeberger, Matthäus (1501-
    1559), 9n.
Red Sea, deliverance at, 169
Reform Judaism, musical prac-
    tices in, 177, 184
Reformed Devotions (Hickes),
    117-118
Reformed Presbyterian Church,
    musical rules of, 18
Requiem (Fauré, 1887), 22
Requiem (Verdi; tribute to the
    patriot, Manzoni, 1874), 22
Revolution, American, 100
Rhau, Georg (1488-1548; can-
    tor at the Thomasschule,
    Leipzig, until 1520; printer
    at Wittenberg after 1525),
    10n.
Richter, Jean Paul (1763-1825),
    73
Rimbault, Edward F. (1816-
    1876), 25n.

Rinaldo (1711), 78
Ripping Up of the Pope's Fardel,
    The (1581), 38
"Rock of Ages" (Augustus M.
    Toplady, 1776), 148, 155,
    160
Romaine, William (1714-1795),
    95n., 99n.
Roman Catholic church music
    (16th century), 3, 14-15,
    27
Roman choirs, performance
    standards of, 176n.
Roméo et Juliette (1867), 173
Rosh Hashanah mode, 181
Rossetti, Dante Gabriel (1828-
    1882), 102
Rossi, Salomone (1587-1628),
    182
Rouault, Georges (b. 1871), 174
Rous, Francis (1579-1659), 20
Rubbra, Edmund Duncan (b.
    1901), 175n.
Rubinstein, Anton (1829-1894),
    182
Rubio, Samuel P., 176n.
Rubsamen, Walter (b. 1911),
    185n.
Runyan, W. R., 159n.
Rupff, Conrad, 8

S. P. G., see Society for the
    Propagation of the Gospel
Sabaneëv, Leonid (b. 1881),
    183
Sackville College, 143
Sacred Oratorio, A, see Messiah
Sadoleto, Jacopo, Cardinal
    (1477-1547), 22-23
St. Anne (hymn-tune ascribed to
    William Croft), 180
St. Bartholomew's massacre
    (1572), 20n.
Saint Cecilia Mass (1882), 173

St. George's Chapel (Windsor), 30, 32, 39
St. John Passion (1723), 67
St. Mark's (Venice), 50
St. Matthew Passion (1729), 44, 52, 65, 67, 77
St. Patrick's (Dublin), 84
St. Paul's (London), 39, 138
St. Paul's Within-the-Walls (Rome), 159
St. Thomas Church, Leipzig, see Thomaskirche
St. Thomas School, Leipzig, see Thomasschule
Saintsbury, George (1845-1933), 111
Salvation Songs and Solos (Sankey), 151
Salzburgers, doubts concerning baptism of, 125
Samson (1743), 85, 87-90
Samson Agonistes (Milton), 87
Samuel, I, Sermons on Book of, (Calvin), 14
Sanctus (Lutheran liturgy), 50
Sandys, George (1578-1644), 121
Sankey, David (father of Ira), 154
Sankey, Ira D. (1840-1908), 151-162
Saturday Review of Literature, quotation from (June 29, 1946), 173
Saul, first king of Israel, 9
Saul (1739), 82, 90
Savannah (Georgia)
    Grand Jury charges against Wesley, 120
    "second rise of Methodism," (April, 1736), 115
Saxony, 60, 71
Scheibe, Johann A. (1708-1776; music critic in Hamburg after 1736), 42n.

Schönberg, Arnold (1874-1951), 182, 185
Schola[e] Cantorum, importance of, 168
Scholes, Percy A. (b. 1877), 16n., 21n., 38
Schütz, Heinrich (1585-1672), 11
Schumann, Robert (1810-1856), 73
Schweitzer, Albert (b. 1875), 10, 46, 47n., 48n., 68
Scott, Sir Walter (1771-1832), 125
Seatonian Poetry Prize, 145
Senesino, Francesco (1680-1750?), 78
Senfl, Ludwig (1490?-1543; court chapelmaster at Munich from 1523-1540), 5, 11, 45
Shaftesbury, Earl of (Cooper, Anthony Ashley [1801-1885]; noted philanthropist), 152
"Shine, Mighty God, on Britain" (Watts's Psalm LXVII), 98
Shuster, George, 169n.
Sidon, 58
"Sing to the Lord with Joyful Voice" (Watts), 98
Singing of Psalmes a Gospel-Ordinance (Cotton, 1647), 17
Siroe (1728), 79
Six Articles, see Act Abolishing Diversity in Opinions
Society for the Propagation of the Gospel, 126, 128
Solomon (1749), 89
Song of Solomon, 52, 74
Songs of Praise Discussed, 141
South Carolina, early printing in, 126

South Carolina Gazette, 127
Southwark, 36
Spener, Philipp Jacob (1635-1705; Pietist leader), 47, 51n.
Spitta, Philipp (1841-1894), 44n., 50n., 51n.
Stabat Mater (Palestrina), 22
Stebbins, George Coles (1846-1945), 158-159
Stenger, Nikolaus (1638-1686; author of *Grundfeste der Augspurg-Confession*), 74
Sternhold and Hopkins (metrical psalter), 20, 116, 120
Stieglitz, Christian Ludwig, burgomaster of Leipzig, 64, 68, 70-71, 75
Story of American Catholicism, The, 169n.
Stradella, Alessandro (1645-1682), 83
Stravinsky, Igor (b. 1882), 175
Strype, John (1643-1737), 28
Stuart, Moses, 73n., 74n.
Sumner, Charles (1790-1874; bishop of Winchester), 143
Susanna, 89
Susanna (1749), 67, 89
Swift, Jonathan (1667-1745), 78, 84
syllabic type melodies, Cranmer's favoring of, 26
synagogue[s], hymns of Christian provenience inappropriate for, 178
Syntagma Musicum (1615-1620), 8

Tallis, Thomas (1505?-1585), 138
Tate, Nahum (1652-1715), 180
Tate and Brady (metrical psalter), 116, 120-121

Bishop of London's recommendation of, 120
Neale's distaste for, 147
Wesley's opinion of, 120
Tauler, Johann (1300?-1361; mystic), 51n.
Taverner, John (1495?-1545), 39-40
Taylor, Sedley, 83n.
Te Deum, 172n.
Telemann, Georg Philipp (1681-1767), 42
Telford, John, 120n., 134n.
Temple, The (Herbert), 123
Teresa, Saint, 104n.
Terry, Charles Sanford (1864-1936), 43n., 46n., 49n., 55n., 57n.
Terry, Sir Richard Runciman (1865-1938), 29, 30n., 38n., 39n., 40n., 165n.
Tersteegen, Gerhard (1697-1769), 125
Testem Benevolentiae (Leo XIII's encyclical), 176
Testwood, Robert, 32-33, 37
Theodora (1750), 67, 91
"The God of Abraham Praise" (Thomas Olivers' paraphrase, *ca.* 1770), 179n.
"The Ninety and Nine" (music by Sankey), 151
"The Royal Banners Forward Go" (Venantius Fortunatus, 569), 140
"The Spacious Firmament on High" (Addison, 1712), 140
"There Is a Fountain Filled With Blood" (Cowper), 160
Thomasius, Christian (1655-1728), 50
Thomas, Isaiah (1749-1831), 128n.

Thomaskirche (Leipzig), 49, 61, 69

Thomasschule (Leipzig), 43-44, 50, 64, 68-69, 76

Thomson, Virgil (b. 1896), 184

"Thou, Lord, My Power and Wisdom Art" (Herbert), 124

Tillotson, John (1630-1694; Archbishop of Canterbury), 128

Timothy, Lewis (d. 1738), 126-127

Timothy, Peter (son of Lewis), 126, 128

title, Bach's hankering after, 63-64

Tolomeo (1728), 79

Toplady, Augustus M. (1740-1778), 148

Torgau (Saxony), 8, 11-12

Towle, Eleanor A., 142n., 143n., 145n., 149n.

Tractarian musical taste, 28-29

Treviso (Italy), 167

Trinity College (Hartford, Conn.), 148

Trinity (hymn-tune by Felice de Giardini), 180

Triumphant Reigne of Henry VIII, The, 34

Trophimus (Acts 21:29), 59

Turner, Richard (d. 1565; Merbecke's friend), 31

Tye, Christopher (1499-1573), 39-40

Tyre, 58

Union Hymnal
first edition (1897), 177, 179
second edition (1914), 179-180
third edition (1932), 180 *et seq.*

United Presbyterian Church,

organs permitted (1872), 18

Unitas Fratrum, *see* Moravians

"Unto Us a Son Is Given" (*Messiah*), 83

Urban VIII, Pope (1568-1644; issued latest Breviary revision, 1631), 150

Urio, Francesco Antonio (1660-1720?; Franciscan friar and composer), 83

usury, Watts's opinions on, 97

Vannutelli, Vincent, Cardinal (1836-1930), 170n.

Vaughan Williams, R., *see* Williams, Ralph Vaughan

Venantius Fortunatus, *see* Fortunatus, Venantius

Venice, 50, 167

Verdi, Giuseppe (1813-1901), 22

Victoria, Queen (reigned 1837-1901), 152

Virgil, 96n., 102

Vom Himmel Hoch (Luther, 1535), 45

Waldensians, 159

Walpole, Sir Edward (d. 1784), 131n.

Walther, Johann (1496-1570; edited first Protestant sing-ing-book, 1524), 8

Warsaw, 63

Washington *Post*, 173

Watts, Isaac, Dr. (1674-1748), 93-111
"errors in doctrine," 146
popularity in denominational hymnals, 139-140
psalm-imitations favored by Wesley, 120-122
representation in *Union Hymnal*, 180

Webb, Benjamin (1819-1885; ecclesiologist), 145, 148

Wedderburn brothers (James, John, Robert), compilers of *Gude and Godlie Ballates*, 124

Wellesley, Garret (1735-1781; D. Mus., 1764; father of Duke of Wellington), 132n.

Well-Tempered Clavier (Bach), 69, 136

Wesley, Charles (1707-1788; hymnist), 130-132
  accompanies John on Georgia trip, 124
  co-operates in preparing 1784 Collection, 114
  representation in denominational hymnals, 139-140
  reproached by his son, 136
  "right Promethean fire" of, 130
  Whitefield changes first line of "Hark! the Herald Angels Sing," 150

Wesley, Charles (1757-1834; son of preceding), 133

Wesley, John (1703-1791), 112-130
  approves *Messiah*, 85
  attends nephews' concert, 132
  heart "strangely warmed," 112 *et seq.*
  rebukes Watts's "fondling" of Divinity, 104
  views on Watts's theology, 109-110

Wesley, Samuel (1662-1735; rector of Epworth; father of John), 120

Wesley, Samuel (1691-1739; eldest son of Samuel preceding), 124

Wesley, Samuel (1766-1837; son of Charles Wesley,

hymnwriter; foremost English organist of his time)
  embraces Roman Catholicism, 134-135
  opinions on Gregorian chant, and on Bach, 136
  repents choice of music as a career, 136-137
  rescues Handel's hymn-tunes, 133-134

Wesley, Samuel Sebastian (1810-1876; natural son of preceding)
  morning and evening services of, 138
  greatest musical light of Wesley family, 137
  pre-eminence among English composers, 133

Wesley, Susannah (mother of John), 123

West, George John (1791-1869; 5th Earl De La Warr), 143

Westminster Abbey, removal of organs from, 16

Westminster Assembly (1643), 16

"When I Survey the Wondrous Cross" (Watts, 1707), 111n.

"While Shepherds Watched Their Flocks by Night" (Tate, 1700), 180

"Whip with Six Strings" (1539), 30

Whitefield, George (1714-1770), 127, 150

Whitefield hymnbook (1st edition, 1753), 148

Whitmarsh (early Carolina printer), 129n.

Whittier, John Greenleaf (1807-1892), 180

"Why Does the God of Israel Sleep?" (*Samson*), 88

William III (reigned 1689-
    1702)
  Glorious Revolution by, 98
  landing of (November 5,
    1688), 104
  Tate and Brady version com-
    piled during reign of, 116
Williams, Ralph Vaughan (b.
    1872; Mass in G Minor
    composed in 1923), 175n.
Winchester, 34, 144
Windsor Chapel, 39
Wittenberg, 6
Wolsey, Thomas, Cardinal
    (1475?-1530), 86
Wooldridge, H. E. (1845-1917),
    19n., 26n.
Wordsworth, Christopher, Bishop
    (1807-1885), 180
Wyclif, John (1320?-1384), 8

Xenophon, 87

Yattendon Hymnal, 19
"Ye Priests of God, Whose
    Happy Days" (Samuel
    Wesley's Psalm CXIII para-
    phrase), 121
"Yet There Is Room" (Bonar),
    152, 156
Yigdal (Daniel Ben Judah, 14th
    century), 179n.
Yom Kippur mode, 181
York (England), Moody and
    Sankey at, 156
Young, Percy M., 91n.

Zechariah, 86
Zinzendorf, Nikolaus Ludwig,
    Count (1700-1760), 125
Zürich, 3
Zwingli, Huldreich (1484-
    1531), 3, 4, 10